John Phin

The workshop companion. A collection of useful and reliable recipes, rules, processes, methods, wrinkles, and practical hints for the household and the shop

John Phin

The workshop companion. A collection of useful and reliable recipes, rules, processes, methods, wrinkles, and practical hints for the household and the shop

ISBN/EAN: 9783337156688

Printed in Europe, USA, Canada, Australia, Japan

Cover: Foto ©Lupo / pixelio.de

More available books at **www.hansebooks.com**

THE
WORKSHOP COMPANION.

A COLLECTION OF

USEFUL AND RELIABLE RECIPES, RULES, PROCESSES,
METHODS, WRINKLES, AND PRACTICAL HINTS

For the Household and the Shop.

NEW YORK:
THE INDUSTRIAL PUBLICATION COMPANY.
1887.

Copyright secured according to Act of Congress, 1879.

PREFACE.

The following pages have been prepared with very great care, the chief aim being to give none but recipes which will not disappoint those who attempt to use them. Several of the recipes here given are original, the formulæ having been worked out or improved by the author after much labor and experiment. In searching for really good formulæ, we have been astonished at the errors which have crept into many of our standard books of recipes. For example, in one case the two separate operations of a well-known process for staining wood are given as distinct, and, of course useless recipes! In a seemingly favorite recipe for a washing fluid, the reader is directed to add vinegar to the ammonia employed, thus entirely neutralizing it. In the same way we find a recipe for transferring printed engravings to wood, in which the alkali (potash) is neutralized with vitriol! We suppose that in the last case, the author of this recipe thought that *two* strong liquids must be better than one, forgetting or not knowing the fact that one destroys the effect of the other. A very slight knowledge of technological science would have enabled the compilers of these books to avoid such blunders. In addition to these defects, however, most of our large books of recipes contain so much that is entirely useless to the practical man, and so many mere repetitions of the same recipe in different language and terms, that their cost is greatly increased while their value instead of being enhanced, is actually lessened. We have, therefore, endeavored to combine in the following pages all that is really of practical value to the professional or amateur mechanic, and at the same time by giving only one or two of the best recipes under each head, we have not only simplified the work, but we have brought it to such a size and price that every one can afford to buy it.

The subjects treated of in this work are arranged alphabetically, so as to avoid the necessity of constant reference to the index. A few words in regard to the method pursued in arranging the matter may, however, not be out of place. As we believe that the greatest advantage will be derived from bringing together at one place not only the special instructions in regard to particular processes, but the general information relating to the materials, etc., employed, we have in most cases collected all such matter together under one head. Thus, under the head of "Steel" will be found not only a description of the different kinds of steel, but directions for forging, tempering, etc., but as most persons who consult this book would most likely look under the head "Tempering" for information on that particular subject, we have entered the word "Tempering" and under it give a cross-reference to "Steel." This is the reason why we have introduced so many cross references, every one of which was put in *after* the book was written, so that the reader will not be disappointed when he turns to the heading to which he is directed. Many of our readers, doubtless, know that in too many volumes of this kind, cross references are inserted merely for the purpose of swelling the apparent amount of information contained in the volume, and very often when the reader turns to the heading to which he is directed, he finds that the subject which he is looking for has been omitted. In the present case, the utmost care has been taken to prevent disappointment of every kind, and whenever information is promised we have endeavored to give it fully, accurately, and in the simplest possible language.

J. P.

New York, Nov. 1879.

THE
WORKSHOP COMPANION.

Abyssinian Gold.
This compound was so called because it was brought out in England during the recent war with Abyssinia. It consists of copper, 90·74; zinc, 8·33. This alloy, if of good materials and not heated too highly, has a fine yellow color, resembling gold, and does not tarnish easily.

Accidents.
As those who are engaged in mechanical pursuits are peculiarly liable to accidents, we have introduced under the proper heads (Burns, Eye, Fires, Poisons) such brief suggestions as we thought might prove valuable to our readers. For more minute directions in regard to drowning, severe cuts, gunshot wounds, sprains, dislocations, etc., we must refer the reader to some one of the numerous treatises which have been published on this subject*. The following general rules will be found useful in all cases:

General Rules. 1. The first thing to be done in all cases is to send for a physician. While the messenger is gone, endeavor to make the patient as comfortable as possible, and save him from all exertion, remembering that he needs all his strength. 2. If there be any severe bleeding, stanch the blood by means of compresses applied to the veins or arteries, as the case may be. 3. If the patient be insensible, place him on the ground or floor, lying rather over to or directly on one side, and with the head slightly raised. Remove necktie, collar, etc., and unbutton or split open any clothing pressing

---

*One of the best is that issued by the publishers of this volume. It is entitled "What to Do and How to Do it in Case of Accident." Price 30 cents.

tightly upon the neck, chest, or abdomen. 4. As a restorative, sprinkle the face with cold water, and then wipe it dry. Some cold water may be given to drink, if the power of swallowing be present, but do not pour stimulants down the throat, unless there be clear evidence that they are needed. 5. Do not move the patient, unless to get him to a place of shelter, and when he has reached it, make him lie down and seek quiet. 6. Allow no useless talking, either to the patient, or in his presence. 7. Cause the bystanders to move back and leave a clear space of at least ten feet in every direction around the patient. One of the best restoratives is fresh air, and a crowd cuts this off completely.

Stimulants should be avoided, except in cases urgently demanding their administration, but they are agents of much value in the treatment of that condition of collapse and faintness which very commonly occurs after some physical injuries. The symptoms may be briefly sketched: The face is pale and bedewed with cold or clammy perspiration; the surface of the body generally cold; the pulse flickering, perhaps hardly perceptible; the patient complains of the feeling of faintness, and may have nausea, or even actual sickness; the breathing is sighing and irregular, and for a time there may be actual insensibility. Now under such conditions there can be no question as to the propriety of inducing reaction by the administration of stimulants.

Coffee given hot and strong, and in small quantities, is a safe and useful remedy.

Spirituous liquors are more potent in their effects, and the good effect is produced more speedily. Brandy is the best spirit, given in more or less diluted form; failing this, rum or wine may be given. If the spirits can be obtained only from some low grog shop, then whiskey is to be preferred to brandy or wine, as being less liable to adulteration. In administering these articles the best practical rule is to give a small quantity at first and watch the effect; if the surface becomes warmer, the breathing deeper and more regular, and the pulse at the wrist more perceptible, then there can be no question as to the advantage of giving even a little more; but if these signs of improvement are wanting—if there be increase of insensibility, and deepening of color about the face, with access of heat of skin—withhold alcohol entirely; it will but add to the mischief.

Alabaster.

This material is so common and yields such beautiful results when worked, that a few hints in regard to working and mending it may not be out of place.

There are two distinct chemical compounds to which the name of alabaster has been applied, the most common being the sulphate of lime, while that known as *oriental alabaster* is a stalagmitic carbonate of lime, compact or fibrous, generally white, but of all colors from white to brown, and sometimes veined with colored zones; it is of the same hardness as marble, is used for similar purposes, and is wrought by the same means.

Of the common alabaster (sulphate of lime) there are several varieties. The finest white alabaster is obtained from Italy, but very excellent specimens are found near Derby in England. (They must not, however, be confounded with Derbyshire or fluor spar which is a calcic fluoride.) The variegated kinds are turned into pillars, vases and various ornamental forms, the tools used being very simple, namely, points for roughing out, flat chisels for smoothing, and one or two common firmer chisels, ground convex and concave for curved lines. After being brought to the proper shape, the work is polished as follows: Take a piece of very fine, soft sandstone, and apply it with water to the work while in quick motion, moving the stone all over until there is worked up a body of mud. Then take a clean rag and work this sludge well on the alabaster, after which wash the work clean. Apply a rag charged with putty powder and water until there is a gloss upon the work, after which apply another rag charged with a mixture of putty powder, soap and water for a short time, and wipe the alabaster dry. If carefully performed the polish will be very beautiful.

Alabaster readily absorbs grease and dirt, and as it is difficult to clean, great care should be taken to prevent it from coming in contact with anything that will stain it. Dust, etc., may be removed by means of pure water to which a little ammonia has been added. Grease and similar stains may be removed by allowing the alabaster to lie for some time in contact with a paste of powdered chalk moistened with a solution of potash or soda. Soap should never be used for cleaning alabaster, as it leaves a greasy stain. Unlike marble, alabaster is not affected by common acids, and therefore they may be used for extracting stains of common ink, etc.

The proper cement for uniting pieces of alabaster is plaster of paris made into a cream with water as for making ordinary casts. The surfaces to be joined must be moistened with water.

Alcohol.

This familiar liquid requires no description, but it may not be out of place to caution our readers that failure in the making of varnishes, etc., very often arises from the use of alcohol which by standing has lost its strength. Ordinary alcohol is a mixture of alcohol and water, and as the alcohol evaporates more readily than the water, when the mixture is allowed to stand for any length of time it becomes reduced in strength, that is to say the proportion of alcohol becomes less and that of the water more.

Alloys.

In making alloys, especially where the component metals vary greatly in fusibility and volatility, the following rules must be observed:

1. Melt the least fusible, oxidable and volatile first, and then add the others heated to their point of fusion or near it. Thus if we desire to make an alloy of exactly one part copper and three zinc, it will be impossible to do so by putting these proportions of the metals in a crucible and exposing the whole to heat. Much of the zinc would fly off in vapor before the copper was melted. First melt the copper and add the zinc which has been melted in another crucible. The zinc should be in excess, as some of it will be lost anyway.

2. Some alloys, as copper and zinc, copper and arsenic, may be formed by exposing heated plates of the least fusible metal to the vapor of the other. In making brass in the large way, thin plates of copper are dissolved as it were in melted zinc until the proper proportions have been obtained.

3. The surface of all oxidable metals should be covered with some protecting agent, as tallow for very fusible ones; resin for lead and tin; charcoal for zinc, copper, etc.

4. Stir the metal before casting, and, if possible, when casting, with a whitewood stick; this is much better for the purpose than an iron rod.

5. If possible, add a small portion of old alloy to the new one. If the alloy is required to make sharp castings, and strength is not a very great object, the proportion of old alloy to the new should be increased. In all cases a new or thoroughly well cleaned crucible should be used.

Albata.—Known also as "British plate," "electrum," etc. It is a favorite material for making articles that are to be electrotyped. The best proportions of the ingredients are copper, 20; nickel, 4; zinc, 16.

Alloy for filling holes in Iron.—Lead, 9; antimony, 2; bismuth, 1. This alloy is sometimes called "mock iron;" it expands in cooling, so that when a hole is filled with the melted alloy, the plug is not loose when it is cold.

Alloy for Uniting Iron, Steel and Brass.—The following composition may be cast on steel or iron, and will adhere firmly thereto. Its rate of expansion is nearer that of iron and steel than any similar compound. When cast around iron or steel therefore, it closes firmly around them and does not become loose by alternate expansion and contraction. It consists of tin, 3; copper, $39\frac{1}{2}$; zinc, $7\frac{1}{4}$. Since the last metal is partly converted into vapor at a high temperature, the above proportion may be slightly increased.

Aluminium Bronze.—Copper, 90; aluminium, 10. Resembles gold in color, and is very strong and durable.

Aluminium Silver.—Copper, 70; nickel, 23; aluminium, 7. Has a beautiful color and takes a high polish.

Amalgam for Silvering the insides of Globes, etc.—1. Lead, 2 oz.; tin, 2 oz.; bismuth, 2 oz.; mercury, 4 oz. Melt the first three and add the mercury. The glass being well cleaned, is carefully warmed and the melted amalgam is poured in and the vessel turned round until all parts are coated. At a certain temperature this amalgam adheres readily to glass.

2. Bismuth, 8; lead, 5; tin, 3; mercury, 8. Use as directed for No. 1.

Amalgam for Electrical Machines.—1. Tin, 1 oz.; zinc, 1 oz.; mercury, 2 oz.

2. *Bœttger's Amalgam.*—Zinc, 2 oz.; mercury, 1 oz. At a certain temperature (easily found by experiment) it powders readily, and should be kept in a tightly corked bottle. Said to be very good.

Cock Metal.—Copper, 10; lead, 4. Used for casting cocks.

Copper Amalgam.—Dissolve 3 oz. sulphate of copper in

water and add 1 oz. sulphuric acid. Hang clean iron scraps in the solution until the copper has fallen down in fine powder. Wash this powder, moisten it with a solution of protonitrate of mercury, and then to each ounce of the powder add 2½ oz. mercury, and rub up in a mortar. When thoroughly mixed, wash well with hot water. This amalgam is easily moulded, adheres readily to glass, porcelain and some metals, takes a fine polish, and in 10 to 12 hours it becomes so hard that it will scratch gold or tin. When heated it softens, and may be easily moulded. As it does not contract on cooling, it has been used by dentists for filling teeth, and it might be used to good advantage for inlaying lines in dark wood.

Protonitrate of mercury is easily made by dissolving mercury in nitric acid.

Babbitt's Anti-Attrition Metal for lining Boxes.—First melt four pounds of copper, and, when melted, add, by degrees, twelve pounds best quality Banca tin; then add eight pounds regulus of antimony, and then twelve pounds more of tin, while the composition is in a melted state. After the copper is melted and four or five pounds of tin have been added, the heat should be lowered to a dull red heat, in order to prevent oxidation; then add the remainder of the metal. In melting the composition it is better to keep a small quantity of powdered charcoal in the pot, on the surface of the metal.

The above composition is made in the first place, and is called hardening; for lining work take one pound of the hardening and melt with two pounds Banca tin, which produces the very best lining metal. So that the proportions for lining metal are four pounds copper, eight regulus of antimony and ninety-six pounds tin.

The object in first preparing the hardening is economy, for when the whole is melted together there is a great waste of metal, as the hardening is melted at a much less degree of heat than the copper and antimony separately.

Belgian Antifriction Metals.—For work exposed to great heat: Copper, 17; zinc, 1; tin, 0·5; lead, 0·25.

For parts liable to much concussion: Copper, 20; zinc, 6; tin, 1.

For parts exposed to much friction: Copper, 20; tin, 4; antimony, 0·5; lead, 0·25.

Cheap Antifriction Metal.—Equal parts of zinc and lead

melted together, and well stirred at the time of pouring into the box or bearing.

Fusible Metals.—These are chiefly used as a means of amusement, spoons formed of them melting readily in hot tea or coffee. They have also been used to make plugs for steam boilers, the intention being that they should melt and allow the steam to escape when the pressure became too great. No. 4 has been used for making casts of coins and medals, and the beautiful French cliché moulds were made of it.

1. Newton's fusible metal: Bismuth, 8; lead, 5; tin, 3. Melts with the heat of boiling water.
2. Onion's metal: Lead, 3; tin, 2; bismuth, 5. Melts at 197 degrees, Fahrenheit.
3. Wood's fusible metal: Bismuth, 15; lead, 8; tin, 4; cadmium, 3. Melts between 150 and 160 deg. Fahr.
4. Cliché metal: Bismuth, 8; tin, 4; lead, 5; antimony, 1. The metals should be repeatedly melted together and poured into drops or granulated, until they are well mixed.

Pewter.—Tin, 4; lead 1. Old articles of pewter form therefore, a very fine metal for solder.

Queen's Metal.—Tin, 100; antimony, 8; copper, 4; bismuth, 1. Resembles silver in appearance.

Speculum Metal.—Copper, 32; tin, 15; arsenic, 2. First melt the copper, and then add the tin which should have been melted in a separate crucible. Mix thoroughly and add the arsenic.

Type Metal.—Lead, 44; antimony 8; tin, 1.

Amber.

Amber is principally obtained from the shores of the Baltic, but it is also found in other parts of Europe. The most esteemed is the opaque variety, resembling the color of a lemon, and sometimes called fat amber; the transparent pieces are very brittle and vitreous. The German pipe makers, by whom it is principally used, employ thin scraping tools, and they burn a small lamp or place a little pan of burning charcoal beneath the amber to warm it slightly whilst it runs in the lathe. This prevents it from chipping out, but if it is too highly heated by friction it is apt to fly to pieces.

The finer specimens of amber, which are sometimes formed into gems and ornaments, are ground on lead plates made to revolve in the lathe, any of the usual abrasive substances (sand or emery) being used. The facets are then finished by means of a whetstone, and polished with chalk mixed with water or vegetable oil. The final finish is given by means of flannel. During the polishing process the amber becomes very warm and highly electric, and if this heating goes too far it will fly in pieces. The workmen, therefore, cool it off every now and then.

Amber, to Unite Broken Pieces.—Coat with linseed oil the surfaces that are to be joined; hold the oiled parts carefully over a charcoal fire, a few hot cinders or a gaslight, being careful to cover up all the rest of the object loosely with paper. When the oiled parts have begun to feel the heat so as to be sticky, press and clamp them together and keep them so until nearly cold. Only that part where the edges are to be united must be warmed, and even that with care lest the form or polish of the other parts should be disturbed; the part where the joint occurs generally requires to be repolished.

Imitation Amber.—Of late, an imitation of amber, which cannot be distinguished from the genuine article by inspection, has made its appearance on the market. It contains copal, camphor, turpentine, and other ingredients, becomes electric by friction, and is used for manufacturing mouth-pieces for pipes, cigar-holders, ornaments, etc. The composition may be distinguished from genuine amber by its lower melting point, as it quickly softens and melts when laid on a hot plate, while amber requires a comparatively high heat; and further by the action of ether, which softens the imitation until it may be scraped away with the finger-nail, while true amber is absolutely insoluble in cold ether.

Annealing and Hardening.

For the best methods of annealing, hardening and tempering steel, see article STEEL in this volume. Several valuable facts in regard to glass are also given under GLASS.

Copper, brass, German silver and similar metals are hardened by hammering, rolling or wire drawing, and are softened by being heated red hot and plunged in water. Copper, by being alloyed with tin, may be made so hard that cutting instruments may be made of it. This is the old process of hardening copper, which is so often claimed to be one of the lost arts, and which would be very useful if we did not have in steel a material which is far less costly and far better fitted for the making of edge tools.

Antiseptic Preparations.

Specimens of natural history intended for subsequent examination and dissection are best preserved in alcohol, but as this is expensive, a saturated solution of 100 parts of alum and 2 parts of saltpetre may be used with good effect. For preserving stuffed specimens the following are generally used:

Arsenical Soap.—This is the most powerful preservative in use. It is a strong poison, but is invaluable for preserving skins of birds and beasts that are to be stuffed. It is made thus: Powdered arsenic, 2 oz.; camphor, 5 oz.; white soap, 2 oz.; salt of tartar (sub-carbonate of potash), 6 drachms; powdered lime, 2 drachms. Cut the soap in very thin slices and heat gently with a small quantity of water, stirring all the time with a stick. When thoroughly melted add the salt of tartar and the lime. When these are well mixed together add the arsenic, which must be carefully incorporated with the other ingredients. Take the mixture off the fire, and while cooling add the camphor, previously reduced to powder by rubbing it with a little alcohol. When finished the soap should be of the consistence of thick cream and should be kept in a tightly stopped bottle.

Arsenical Preservative Powder.—This is dusted over moist skins and flesh, and preserves almost any animal matter from putrefaction. It is thus made: Arsenic, 4 oz.; burnt alum, 4 oz.; tanner's bark, 8 oz; mix and grind together to a very fine powder.

Beeswax.

Beeswax is obtained by washing and melting the honeycomb. The product is yellow and is freed from its impurities, and bleached by melting it with hot water or steam, in a tinned copper or wooden vessel, letting it settle, running it off into an oblong trough with a line of holes in its bottom, so as to distribute it upon horizontal wooden cylinders, made to revolve, half immersed in cold water, and then exposing the thin ribbons or films thus obtained, to the blanching action of air, light, and moisture. For this purpose the ribbons are laid upon long webs of canvas stretched horizontally between standards, two feet above the surface of a sheltered field, having a free exposure to the sunbeams. Here they are frequently turned over, then covered by nets to prevent their being blown away by winds, and watered from time to time, like linen upon the grass field in the old method of bleaching. Whenever the color of the wax seems stationary, it is collected, re-melted, and thrown again into ribbons upon the wet cylinder, in order to expose new surfaces to the bleaching operation. By several repetitions of these processes, if the weather proves favorable, the wax becomes quite white.

Black-boards.

Various kinds of so-called "liquid slating" have been sold for converting any smooth board or wall into a black-board for school or other purposes. The following give very good results; No. 1 is probably the best, but is somewhat expensive.

1. Take alcohol (95 per cent.), 4 pints; shellac, 8 ounces; lamp-black, 12 drachms; ultramarine blue, 20 drachms; powdered rotten stone, 4 ounces; powdered pumice stone, 6 ounces. First dissolve the shellac in the alcohol, then add the other ingredients, finely powdered, and shake well. To apply the slating, have the surface of the board smooth and perfectly free from grease. Shake well the bottle containing the preparation, pour out a small quantity only into an old tea-cup, and apply it with a new flat varnish brush as rapidly as possible. Keep the bottle well corked, and shake it up every time before pouring out the liquid.

2. Instead of alcohol take a solution of borax in water; dissolve the shellac in this and color with lamp-black.

3. Dilute silicate of soda (water-glass) with an equal bulk of water, and add sufficient lamp-black to color it. The lamp-black should be ground with water and a little of the silicate before being added to the rest of the liquid.

Brass.

Next to iron, brass is probably the most generally useful metal, and as the varieties of this alloy are almost infinite, the range of purposes to which it may be applied is very great. The color of the alloy inclines to red when the proportion of zinc is small, gradually changing to yellow, and ultimately white, when the proportion of zinc is very large. The ductility and malleability of the alloy increase with the quantity of copper. Ordinary brass may be hammered, rolled into sheets or drawn to wire while cold, provided it is occasionally annealed by heating it to a very low red heat. When worked hot it crumbles to pieces under the hammer or between the rolls. But the so-called yellow metal, or Muntz metal, an alloy of 40 parts of zinc and 60 of copper, may be wrought while red hot, rolled into sheets and forged into bolts. Brass is not so readily oxidized as copper, being harder, tougher, more easily fusible and more fluid when molten. It solidifies without becoming honey-combed, and hence is suited for making all kinds of castings; while simply by the addition of from 1 to 2 per cent. of lead, it is capable of being readily worked on the lathe, and may then be filed without, as it otherwise does, clogging the teeth of the file.

Finishing Brass.—The article having been brought to proper shape by means of the lathe, file, grindstone or other means, the surface must be rendered smooth and free from lumps, utters, or scratches. If finished in the lathe, emery paper and oil may be used to smooth the surface, the final polish being imparted by rouge. In all cases where brass or other metals are polished by means of abrasive materials, great care must be taken that all corners are left sharp and well-defined, since nothing looks so badly as a corner which ought to be square but which is worn and rounded in the process of polishing.

In finishing brass work (and the same remark applies to the polishing of other materials) great care must be taken to avoid making any scratches which are deeper than the other marks left by the material employed. Such scratches are very difficult to remove by very fine files or by polishing powders, and therefore, whenever the work shows such scratches it is necessary to go back to the coarse file or scraper and begin anew. (See articles on *Polishing Metals* and *Polishing Powders.*)

Coloring and Varnishing Brass.—To prevent the everyday rusting of brass goods, the trade has long resorted to means for protecting the surface from the action of the atmosphere, the first plan of which is to force a change to take place. Thus, if brass is left in damp sand, it acquires a beautiful brown color, which, when polished with a dry brush, remains permanent and requires no cleaning. It is also possible to impart a green and light coating of verdigris on the surface of the brass by means of dilute acids, allowed to dry spontaneously. The antique appearance thus given is very pleasing, and more or less permanent. But it is not always possible to wait for goods so long as such processes require, and hence more speedy methods became necessary, many of which had to be further protected by a coat of varnish. Before bronzing, however, all the requisite fitting is finished, and the brass annealed, pickled in old or dilute nitric acid, till the scales can be removed from the surface, scoured with sand and water, and dried. Bronzing is then performed according to the color desired; for although the word means a brown color, being taken from the Italian "*bronzino*," signifying burnt brown, yet in commercial language it includes all colors. (*See article on Bronzing.*)

Browns of all shades are obtained by immersion in solutions of nitrate or the perchloride of iron; the strength of the solutions determining the depth of the color. Violets are produced by dipping in a solution of chloride of antimony. Chocolate is obtained by burning on the surface of the brass moist red oxide of iron, and polishing with a very small quantity of blacklead.

Olive-green results from making the surface black by means of a solution of iron and arsenic in muriatic acid, the details of the process being as follows:

Make the articles bright, then dip in aqua fortis, which must be thoroughly rinsed off with clean water. Then make the following mixture: Hydrochloric acid, 6 lbs.; sulphate of iron, ¼ lb.; white arsenic, ¼ lb. Be careful to get all the ingredients pure. Let the articles lie in the mixture till black; take out and dry in hot sawdust, polish with blacklead, and lacquer with green lacquer composed of one part lac varnish, four of turmeric, and one of gamboge.

A steel-gray color is deposited on brass from a dilute boiling solution of chloride of arsenic; and a blue by careful treatment with strong hyposulphite of soda.

Black is much used for optical brass work, and is obtained by coating the brass with a solution of platinum, or with chloride of gold mixed with nitrate of tin. The Japanese bronze their brass by boiling it in a solution of sulphate of copper, alum and verdigris.

Success in the art of bronzing greatly depends on circumstances, such as the temperature of the alloy or of the solution, the proportions of the metals used in forming the alloy, and the quality of the materials. The moment at which to withdraw the goods, the drying of them, and a hundred little items of care and manipulation, require attention which experience alone can impart.

To avoid giving any artificial color to brass, and yet to preserve it from becoming tarnished, it is usual to cover properly cleaned brass with a varnish called "lacquer." To prepare the brass for this, the goods, after being annealed, pickled, scoured and washed, as already explained, are either dipped for an instant in pure commercial nitrous acid, washed in clean water, and dried in sawdust, or immersed in a mixture of one part of nitric acid with four of water, till a white curd covers the surface, at which moment the goods are withdrawn, washed in clean water, and dried in sawdust. In the first case the brass will be bright; in the latter, a dead flat which is usually relieved by burnishing the prominent parts. Then the goods are dipped for an instant in commercial nitric acid, and well washed in water containing some argol (to preserve the color till lacquered), and dried in warm sawdust. So prepared, the goods are conveyed to the lacquer room, where they are heated on a hot plate and varnished.

The varnish used is one of spirit, consisting, in its simple form, of one ounce of shellac dissolved in one pint of alcohol. To this simple varnish are added such coloring substances as red sanders, dragon's-blood, and annatto, for imparting richness of color. To lower the tone of color, turmeric, gamboge, saffron, Cape aloes, and sandarac are used. The first group reddens, the second yellows the varnish, while a mixture of the two gives a pleasing orange. (*See article on Lacquer.*)

To Whiten Brass.—Small articles of brass or copper may be whitened by boiling them in a solution of ¾ lb. cream of tartar, 2 quarts of water, and 1 lb. grain tin or any pure tin finely divided. The tin dissolves in the cream of tartar and is again precipitated on the brass or copper.

Depositing Brass by Electricity.—The first step is to thoroughly cleanse the articles, either by means of emery, or by laying them overnight in a weak bath of sulphuric acid. They are then washed off with water, a weak soda solution, and then immersed as the cathode of a bath consisting of 2½ parts of sulphate of copper, 20 parts sulphate of zinc, and 45 parts cyanide of potassium, in 300 parts of water. The anode should be two plates of zinc and copper of equal size. The color of the resulting brass coating may be modified by varying the depth of immersion of one or the other of the plates. The galvanic current should be a strong one, and the liberation of hydrogen bubbles on the object to be brassed should be plentiful. It is important, however, to note that the objects should be first coppered to insure a strong attachment of the brass coating.

Coating Brass with Copper.—The following valuable process for coating brass with copper, is given by Dr. C. Puscher: Dissolve ten parts, by weight, of sulphate of copper, and five of sal-ammoniac, in one hundred and fifty parts, by weight, of water. Place the brass, well cleaned and free from fatty matter on its surface, into this mixture; leave it in it for a minute; let the excess of liquid drain off first, and heat the metal next over a charcoal fire, until the evolution of ammoniacal vapors ceases, and the coppery film appears perfect. Wash with cold water and dry. The coating of copper adheres firmly.

Cleaning Brass.—Large articles of brass and copper which have become very much soiled may be cleaned by a mixture of rotten-stone powder (or any sharp polishing powder) with a strong solution of oxalic acid. After being thoroughly cleaned, the metal should be wiped off with a cloth moistened with soda or potash, and a very light coating of oil should be applied to prevent the further corroding action of the acid.

A more powerful cleaning agent, because very corrosive, is finely powdered bichromate of potash mixed with twice its bulk of strong sulphuric acid and diluted (after standing an hour or so) with an equal bulk of water. This will instantly clean the dirtiest brass, but great care must be taken in handling the liquid, as it is very corrosive.

Brass which has been lacquered should never be cleaned with polishing powders or corrosive chemicals. Wiping with a soft cloth is sufficient, and in some cases washing with weak soap and water may be admissible. Dry the articles thoroughly, taking care not to scratch them, and if, after this, they show much sign of wear or corrosion, send them to the lacquerer to be refinished.

Brazing and Soldering.

The term *soldering* is generally applied when fusible alloys of lead and tin are employed for uniting metals. When hard metals, such as copper, brass or silver are used, the term *brazing* (derived from brass) is more appropriate.

In uniting tin, copper, brass, etc., with any of the soft solders, a copper soldering-iron is generally used. This tool and the manner of using it are too well known to need description. In many cases, however, the work may be done more neatly without the soldering-iron, by filing or turning the joints so that they fit closely, moistening them with the soldering fluid described hereafter, placing a piece of smooth tin-foil between them, tying them together with binding wire, and heating the whole in a lamp or fire till the tin-foil melts. We have often joined pieces of brass in this way so that the joints were quite invisible. Indeed, with good soft solder almost all work may be done over a spirit lamp or even a candle, without the use of a soldering-iron.

More minute directions may be found in the *Young Scientist*, Vol. I, page 56.

Advantage may be taken of the varying degrees of fusibility of solders to make several joints in the same piece of work. Thus, if the first joint has been made with fine tinner's solder, there would be no danger of melting it in making a joint near it with bismuth solder, composed of lead, 4; tin, 4; and bismuth, 1; and the melting point of both is far enough removed from that of a solder composed of lead, 2; tin, 1; and bismuth, 2; to be in no danger of fusion during the use of the latter.

Soft solders do not make malleable joints. To join brass, copper or iron so as to have the joint very strong and malleable, hard solder must be used. For this purpose equal parts of silver and brass will be found excellent, though for iron, copper, or very infusible brass, nothing is better than silver coin rolled out thin, which may be done by any silversmith or dentist. This makes decidedly the toughest of all joints, and as a little silver goes a long way, it is not very expensive.

For most hard solders borax is the best flux. It dissolves any oxides which may exist on the surface of the metal, and protects the latter from the further action of the air, so that the solder is enabled to come into actual contact with the surfaces which are to be joined. For soft solders the best flux is a soldering fluid which may be prepared by saturating hydrochloric acid (spirit of salt) with zinc. The addition of a little sal ammoniac improves it. It is said that a solution of phosphoric acid in alcohol makes an excellent soldering fluid, which has some advantages over chloride of zinc.

In using ordinary tinner's solder for uniting surfaces that are already tinned—such as tinned plate and tinned copper—resin is the best and cheapest flux, but when surfaces of iron, brass or copper that have not been tinned are to be joined by soft solder, the soldering fluid is by far the most convenient. Resin possesses this important advantage over soldering fluid, that it does not induce subsequent corrosion of the article to which it is applied. When acid fluxes have been applied to anything that is liable to rust, it is necessary to see that they are thoroughly washed off with clean warm water and the articles carefully and thoroughly dried.

Oil and powdered resin mixed together make a good flux for tinned articles. The mixture can be applied with a small brush or a swab tied to the end of a stick.

In preparing solders, whether hard or soft, great care is requisite to avoid two faults—a want of uniformity in the melted mass, and a change in the proportions of the constituents by the loss of volatile or oxidable ingredients. Thus, where copper, silver, and similar metals are to be mixed with tin, zinc, etc., it is necessary to melt the more infusible metal first. When copper and zinc are heated together, a large portion of the zinc passes off in fumes. In preparing soft solders, the material should be melted under tallow, to prevent waste by oxidation; and in melting hard solders, the same object is accomplished by covering them with a thick layer of powdered charcoal.

To obtain hard solders of uniform composition, they are generally granulated by pouring them into water through a wet broom. Sometimes they are cast in solid masses and reduced to powder by filing. Silver solders for jewelers are generally rolled into thin plates, and sometimes the soft solders, especially those that are very fusible, are rolled into sheets and cut into narrow strips, which are very convenient for small work that is to be heated by a lamp.

The following simple mode of making solder wire, which is very handy for small work, will be found useful. Take a sheet of stiff writing or drawing paper, and roll it in a conical form, rather broad in comparison with its length. Make a ring of stiff wire, to hold it in, attaching a suitable handle to the ring. The point of the cone may first of all be cut off, to leave an orifice of the size required. When filled with molten solder it should be held above a pail of cold water; and the stream of solder flowing from the cone will congeal as it runs, and form the wire. If held a little higher, so that the stream of solder breaks into drops, before striking the water, it will form handy, elongated "tears" of metal; but, by holding it still higher, each drop forms a thin concave cup or shell, and, as each of these forms have their own peculiar uses in business, many a mechanic will find this hint very useful.

Hard solders are usually reduced to powder either by granulation or filing, and then spread along the joints after being mixed with borax, which has been fused and powdered. It is not necessary that the grains of solder should be placed *between* the pieces to be joined, as with the aid of the borax they will "sweat" into the joint as soon as fusion takes place. The same is true of soft solder applied with soldering fluid. One of the essential requisites of success, however, is that the surfaces be clean, bright, and free from all rust.

The best solder for platinum is fine gold. The joint is not only very infusible, but it is not easily acted upon by common agents. For German-silver joints, an excellent solder is composed of equal parts of silver, brass, and zinc. The proper flux is borax.

Bronzing.

Two distinct processes have had this name applied to them. The first consists in staining brass work a dark brown or bronze color and lacquering it; the second consists in partially corroding the brass so as to give it that greenish hue which is peculiar to ancient brass work. The first is generally applied to instruments and apparatus, the second to articles of ornament.

Bronze for Brass Instruments.—1. The cheapest and simplest is undoubtedly a light coat of plumbago or black lead. After brushing the article with plumbago place it on a clear fire till it is made too hot to be touched. Apply a plate brush as soon as it ceases to be hot enough to burn the brush. A few strokes of the brush will produce a dark brown polish approaching black, but entirely distinct from the well known appearance of black lead. Lacquer with any desired tint.

2. Plate powder or rouge may be used instead of plumbago, and gives very beautiful effects.

3. Make the articles clean, bright and free from oil or grease, then dip in aqua fortis, which must be thoroughly rinsed off with clean warm water. Then make the following mixture: Hydrochloric acid, 6 lbs.; sulphate of iron, ½ ib.; white arsenic, ¼ lb. Be careful to get all the ingredients pure. Let the articles lie in the mixture till black, take out and dry in hot sawdust, polish with black lead, and lacquer with green lacquer.

Antique Bronze.—Dissolve 1 oz. sal-ammoniac, 3 oz. cream tartar, and 6 oz. common salt in 1 pint of hot water; add 2 oz. nitrate of copper dissolved in ¼ pint of water; mix well, and, by means of a brush, apply it repeatedly to the article, which should be placed in a damp situation.

Bronzing Liquid.—Dissolve 10 parts of fuchsine and 5 parts of aniline-purple in 100 parts of 95 per cent. alcohol on a water bath; after solution has taken place, add 5 parts of benzoic acid, and keep the whole boiling for 5 or 10 minutes, until the green color of the mixture has given place to a fine light bronze-brown. This liquid may be applied to all metals, as well as many other substances, yields a very brilliant coating, and dries quickly. It is applied with a brush.

Bronzing Wood, Leather, Paper, etc.—1. Dissolve gum lac in four parts by volume of pure alcohol, and then add bronze or any other metal powder in the proportion of one part to three parts of the solution. The surface to be covered must be very smooth. In the case of wood, one or several coats of Mendon or Spanish white are given, and the object is carefully polished. The mixture is painted on, and when a sufficient number of coats have been given, the object is well rubbed. A special advantage of this process is that the coating obtained is not dull, but can be burnished.

2. Another method is to coat the object with copal or other varnish, and when this has dried so far as to become "tacky" dust bronze powder over it. After a few hours the bronzed surface should be burnished with a burnisher of steel or agate.

Browning Gun Barrels. *(See Guns.)*

Burns.

Those who work in red-hot metals, glass blowing, etc., are sometimes apt to burn their fingers. It is well to know that a solution of bicarbonate of soda (baking soda) promptly and permanently relieves all pain. The points to be observed are: 1. Bicarbonate of soda must be used; washing soda and common soda are far too irritant to be applied if the burn is serious. 2. The solution must be saturated. 3. The solution must be ice-cold.

A laboratory assistant in Philadelphia having severely burned the inside of the last joint of his thumb while bending glass tubing, applied the solution of bicarbonate of soda, and not only was the pain allayed, but the thumb could be at once freely used without inconvenience.

Case-Hardening. *(See Iron.)*
Catgut.

This material is so valuable for many purposes that many mechanics will find it useful to know how to make it, as they can then provide themselves with any size and length that may be needed. The process is quite simple. Take the entrails of sheep or other animals, remembering that fat animals afford a very weak string, while those that are lean produce a much tougher article, and thoroughly clean them from all impurities, attached fat, etc. The animal should be newly killed. Wash well in clean water and soak in soft water for two days, or in winter for three days; lay them on a table or board and scrape them with a small plate of copper having a semicircular hole cut in it, the edges of which must be quite smooth and not capable of cutting. After washing put them into fresh water and then let them remain till the next day, when they are to be well scraped. Let them soak again in water for a night, and two or three hours before they are taken out add to each gallon of water 2 oz. of potash. They ought now to scrape quite clean from their inner mucous coat, and will consequently be much smaller in dimensions than at first. They may now be wiped dry, slightly twisted, and passed through a hole in a piece of brass to equalize their size; as they dry they are passed every two or three hours through other holes, each smaller than the last. When dry they will be round and well polished, and after being oiled are fit for use.

Cements.

General Rules.—Some years ago the writer called attention[*] to the fact that quite as much depends upon the manner in which a cement is used as upon the cement itself. The best cement that ever was compounded would prove entirely worthless if improperly applied. The following rules must be vigorously adhered to if success would be secured:

1. Bring the cement into intimate contact with the surfaces to be united. This is best done by heating the pieces to be joined in those cases where the cement is melted by heat, as in using resin, shellac, marine glue, etc. Where solutions are used, the cement must be well rubbed into the surfaces either with a soft brush (as in the case of porcelain or glass), or by rubbing the two surfaces together (as in making a glue joint between two pieces of wood.)

2. As little cement as possible should be allowed to remain between the united surfaces. To secure this the cement should be as liquid as possible (thoroughly melted if used with heat), and the surfaces should be pressed closely into contact (by screws, weights, wedges or cords) until the cement has hardened.

Where the cement is a solution (such as gum in water) and the surfaces are very absorbent (such as porous paper), the surfaces must be *saturated* with cement before they are brought together.

4. Plenty of time should be allowed for the cement to dry or harden, and this is particularly the case in *oil* cements such as copal varnish, boiled oil, white lead, etc. When two surfaces, each half an inch across, are joined by means of a layer of white lead placed between them, six months may elapse before the cement in the middle of the joint has become hard. In such cases a few days or weeks are of no account; at the end of a month the joint will be weak and easily separated, while at the end of two or three years it may be so firm that the material will part anywhere else than at the joint. Hence, where the article is to be used immediately, the only safe cements are those which are liquified by heat and which become hard when cold. A joint made with marine glue is firm an hour after it has been made. Next to cements that are liquified by heat, are those which consist

---

*Technologist, Vol. I (1870), page 188,

of substances dissolved in water or alcohol. A glue joint sets firmly in twenty-four hours; a joint made with shellac varnish becomes dry in two or three days. Oil cements, which do not dry by evaporation, but harden by oxidation (boiled oil, white lead, red lead, etc.), are the slowest of all.

Aquarium Cement.—Litharge; fine, white, dry sand and plaster of paris, each 1 gill; finely pulverized resin, ⅓ gill. Mix thoroughly and make into a paste with boiled linseed oil to which dryer has been added. Beat it well, and let it stand four or five hours before using it. After it has stood for 15 hours, however, it loses its strength. Glass cemented into its frame with this cement is good for either salt or fresh water. It has been used at the Zoölogical Gardens, London, with great success. It might be useful for constructing tanks for other purposes or for stopping leaks.

Armenian Cement.—The jewellers of Turkey, who are mostly Armenians, have a singular method of ornamenting watch cases, etc., with diamonds and other precious stones by simply gluing or cementing them on. The stone is set in gold or silver, and the lower part of the metal made flat or to correspond with that part to which it is to be fixed. It is then warmed gently and the glue applied, which is so very strong that the parts thus cemented never separate. This glue, which will firmly unite bits of glass and even polished steel, and may, of course, be applied to a vast variety of useful purposes, is thus made: Dissolve five or six bits of gum mastic, each the size of a large pea, in as much alcohol as will suffice to render it liquid; in another vessel dissolve as much isinglass, previously a little softened in water, (though none of the water must be used,) in good brandy or rum, as will make a two-ounce phial of very strong glue, adding two small bits of gum galbanum, or ammoniacum, which must be rubbed or ground until they are dissolved. Then mix the whole with a sufficient heat, keep the glue in a phial closely stopped, and when it is to be used set the phial in boiling water. To avoid the cracking of the phial by exposure to such sudden heat, use a thin green glass phial, and hold it in the steam for a few seconds before immersing it in the hot water.

Buckland's Cement.—Finely powdered white sugar, 1 oz.; finely powdered starch, 3 oz.; finely powdered gum arabic, 4 oz. Rub well together in a dry mortar; then little by little add cold water until it is of the thickness of melted glue; put in a wide mouthed bottle and cork closely. The powder, thoroughly ground and mixed, may be kept for any length of time in a wide mouthed bottle, and when wanted a little may be mixed with water with a stiff brush. It answers ordinarily for all the purposes for which mucilage is used, and as a cement for labels it is specially good, as it does not become brittle and crack off.

Casein Mucilage.—Take the curd of skim-milk (carefully freed from cream or oil), wash it thoroughly and dissolve it to saturation in a cold concentrated solution of borax. This mucilage keeps well, and as regards adhesive power far surpasses the mucilage of gum arabic.

Casein and Soluble Glass.—Casein dissolved in soluble silicate of soda or potassa, makes a very strong cement for glass or porcelain.

Cheese Cement for mending China, etc.—Take skim milk cheese, cut it in slices and boil it in water. Wash it in cold water and knead it in warm water several times. Place it warm on a levigating stone and knead it with quicklime. It will join marble, stone or earthenware so that the joining is scarcely to be discovered.

Chinese Cement (Schio-liao).—To three parts of fresh beaten blood are added four parts of slaked lime and a little alum; a thin, pasty mass is produced, which can be used immediately. Objects which are to be made specially water-proof are painted by the Chinese twice, or at the most three times. Dr. Scherzer saw in Pekin a wooden box which had travelled the tedious road via Siberia to St. Petersburg and back, which was found to be perfectly sound and water-proof. Even baskets made of straw became, by the use of this cement, perfectly serviceable in the transportation of oil. Pasteboard treated therewith receives the appearance and strength of wood. Most of the wooden public buildings of China are painted with schio-liao, which gives them an unpleasant reddish appearance, but adds to their durability. This cement was tried in the Austrian department of Agriculture, and by the "Vienna Association of Industry," and in both cases the statements of Dr. Scherzer were found to be strictly accurate.

Chinese Glue.—Shellac dissolved in alcohol. Used for joining wood, earthenware, glass, etc. This cement requires considerable time to become thoroughly hard, and even then is not as strong as good glue. Its portability is its only recommendation.

Faraday's Cup Cement.—Electrical Cement.—Resin, 5 oz.; beeswax 1 oz.; red ochre or Venetian red in powder, 1 oz. Dry the earth thoroughly on a stove at a temperature above 212°. Melt the wax and resin together and stir in the powder by degrees. Stir until cold, lest the earthy matter settle to the bottom. Used for fastening brass work to glass tubes, flasks, etc.

Glass, Earthenware, etc., Cement for.—Dilute white of egg with its bulk of water and beat up thoroughly. Mix to the consistence of thin paste with powdered quicklime. Must be used immediately.

Glass Cement.—Take pulverized glass, 10 parts; powdered fluorspar, 20 parts; soluble silicate of soda, 60 parts. Both glass and fluorspar must be in the finest possible condition, which is best done by shaking each, in fine powder, with water, allowing the coarser particles to deposit, and then to pour off the remainder which holds the finest particles in suspension. The mixture must be made very rapidly, by quick stirring, and when thoroughly mixed must be at once applied. This is said to yield an excellent cement.

Glue is undoubtedly the most important cement used in the arts. Good glue is hard, clear (not necessarily light-colored, however,) and free from bad taste and smell. Glue which is easily dissolved in *cold* water is not strong. Good glue merely swells in cold water and must be heated to the boiling point before it will dissolve thoroughly.

Good glue requires more water than poor, consequently you cannot dissolve six pounds of good glue in the same quantity of water you can six pounds of poor. The best glue, which is clear and red, will require from one-half to more than double the water that is required with poor glue, and the quality of which can be discovered by breaking a piece. If good, it will break hard and tough, and when broken will be irregular on the broken edge. If poor, it will break comparatively easy, leaving a smooth, straight edge.

In dissolving glue, it is best to weigh the glue, and weigh or measure the water. If not done there is a liability of getting more glue than the water can properly dissolve. It is a good plan, when once the quantity of water that any sample of glue will take up has been ascertained, to put the glue and water together at least six hours before heat is applied, and if it is not soft enough then, let it remain longer in soak, for there is no danger of good glue remaining in pure water, even for forty-eight hours.

From careful experiments with dry glue immersed for twenty-four hours in water at 60° Fah., and thereby transformed into a jelly, it was found that the finest ordinary glue, or that made from white bones, absorbs twelve times its weight of water in twenty-four hours; from dark bones, the glue absorbs nine times its weight of water; while the ordinary glue made from animal refuse, absorbs but three to five times its weight of water.

Glue, being an animal substance, it must be kept sweet; to do this it is necessary to keep it cool after it is once dissolved, and not in use. In all cases keep the glue-kettle clean and sweet, by cleansing it often.

Great care must be taken not to burn it, and, therefore, it should always be prepared in a water bath.

Carpenters should remember that fresh glue dries more readily than that which has been once or twice melted.

The advantage of frozen glue is that it can be made up at once, on account of its being so porous. Frozen glue of same grade is as strong as if dried.

If glue is of first-rate quality, it can be used on most kinds of wood work very thin, and make the joint as strong as the original. White glue is only made white by bleaching.

Glue, Liquid.—1. A very strong glue may be made by dissolving 4 oz. of glue in 16 ounces of strong acetic acid by the aid of heat. It is semi-solid at ordinary temperatures, but needs only to be warmed, by placing the vessel containing it into hot water, to be ready for use.

2. Dilute officinal phosphoric acid with two parts, by weight of water, and saturate with carbonate of ammonia; dilute the resulting liquid, which must be still somewhat acid, with another part of distilled water, warm it on a water-bath, and dissolve in it enough good glue to form a thick, syrupy liquid. It must be kept in well-closed bottles.

3. A most excellent form is also *Dumoulin's Liquid and Unalterable Glue.* This is made as follows: Dissolve 8 oz. of best glue in $\frac{1}{2}$ pint of water in a wide-mouthed bottle, by heating the bottle in a water-bath. Then add slowly $2\frac{1}{2}$ oz.

of nitric acid, spec. gr. 1330, stirring constantly. Effervescence takes place under escape of nitrous acid gas. When all the acid has been added, the liquid is allowed to cool. Keep it well corked, and it will be ready for use at any moment. It does not gelatinize, or putrefy or ferment. It is applicable to many domestic uses, such as mending china, wood, etc.

Glue, Mouth.—Good glue, 1 lb.; isinglass, 4 oz. Soften in water, boil and add ¼ lb. fine brown sugar. Boil till pretty thick and pour into moulds.

Glue, Portable.—Put a pinch of shredded gelatine into a wide-mouthed bottle; put on it a very little water, and about one-fourth part of glacial acetic acid; put in a well-fitting cork. If the right quantity of water and acid be used, the gelatine will swell up into worm-like pieces, quite elastic, but at the same time, firm enough to be handled comfortably. The acid will make the preparation keep indefinitely. When required for use, take a small fragment of the swelled gelatine, and warm the end of it in the flame of a match or candle; it will immediately "run" into a fine clear glue, which can be applied at once direct to the article to be mended. The thing is done in half a minute, and is, moreover, done well, for the gelatine so treated makes the very best and finest glue that can be had. This plan might be modified by dissolving a trace of chrome alum in the water used for moistening the gelatine, in which case, no doubt, the glue would become insoluble when set. But for general purposes, there is no need for subsequent insolubility in glue.

Gutta-Percha Cement.—This highly recommended cement is made by melting together, in an iron pan, 2 parts common pitch and 1 part gutta-percha, stirring them well together until thoroughly incorporated, and then pouring the liquid into cold water. When cold it is black, solid, and elastic; but it softens with heat, and at 100° Fahr. is a thin fluid. It may be used as a soft paste, or in the liquid state, and answers an excellent purpose in cementing metal, glass, porcelain, ivory, &c. It may be used instead of putty for glazing windows.

Iron Cement for closing the Joints of Iron Pipes.—Take of coarsely powdered iron borings, 5 pounds; powdered sal ammoniac, 2 oz.; sulphur, 1 oz.; and water sufficient to moisten it. This composition hardens rapidly; but if time can be allowed it sets more firmly without the sulphur. It must be used as soon as mixed and rammed tightly into the joints.

2. Take sal-ammoniac, 2 oz.; sublimed sulphur, 1 oz.; cast-iron filings or fine turnings, 1 lb. Mix in a mortar and keep the powder dry. When it is to be used, mix it with twenty times its weight of clean iron turnings, or filings, and grind the whole in a mortar; then wet it with water until it becomes of convenient consistence, when it is to be applied to the joint. After a time it becomes as hard and strong as any part of the metal.

Japanese Cement.—Paste made of fine rice flour.

Kerosene Oil Lamps.—The cement commonly used for fastening the tops on kerosene lamps is plaster of paris, which is porous and quickly penetrated by the kerosene. Another cement which has not this defect is made with three parts of resin, one of caustic soda and five of water. This composition is mixed with half its weight of plaster of paris. It sets firmly in about three-quarters of an hour. It is said to be of great adhesive power, not permeable to kerosene, a low conductor of heat and but superficially attacked by hot water.

Labels, Cement for.—1. Macerate 5 parts of good glue in 18 parts of water. Boil and add 9 parts rock candy and 3 parts gum arabic.

2. Mix dextrine with water and add a drop or two of glycerine.

3 A mixture of 1 part of *dry* chloride of calcium, or 2 parts of the same salt in the *crystallized* form, and 36 parts of gum arabic, dissolved in water to a proper consistency, forms a mucilage which holds well, does not crack by drying, and yet does not attract sufficient moisture from the air to become wet in damp weather.

4. For attaching labels to tin and other bright metallic surfaces, first rub the surface with a mixture of muriatic acid and alcohol; then apply the label with a very thin coating of the paste, and it will adhere almost as well as on glass.

5. To make cement for attaching labels to metals, take ten parts tragacanth mucilage, ten parts of honey, and one part flour. The flour appears to hasten the drying, and renders it less susceptible to damp. Another cement that will resist the damp still better, but will not adhere if the surface is

greasy, is made by boiling together two parts shellac, one part borax, and sixteen parts water. Flour paste to which a certain proportion of nitric acid has been added, and heat applied, makes a lasting cement, but the acid often acts upon the metals. The acid converts the starch into dextrine.

6. The *Archives of Pharmacy* gives the following recipe for damp-proof mucilage for labels: Macerate five parts of good glue in eighteen to twenty parts of water for a day, and to the liquid add nine parts of rock candy and three parts of gum arabic. The mixture can be brushed upon paper while lukewarm; it keeps well, does not stick together, and, when moistened, adheres firmly to bottles. For the labels of soda or seltzer-water bottles, it is well to prepare a paste of good rye flour and glue, to which linseed-oil, varnish, and turpentine have been added, in the proportion of half an ounce each to the pound. Labels prepared in the latter way do not fall off in damp cellars.

Leather and Metal, Cement for Uniting.—Wash the metal with hot gelatine; steep the leather in an infusion of nut galls (hot) and bring the two together.

Leather Belting, Cement for.—One who has tried everything says that after an experience of fifteen years he has found nothing to equal the following: Common glue and isinglass, equal parts, soaked for 10 hours in just enough water to cover them. Bring gradually to a boiling heat and add pure tannin until the whole becomes ropy or appears like the white of eggs Buff off the surfaces to be joined, apply this cement warm, and clamp firmly.

Litharge and Glycerine Cement.—A cement made of very finely powdered oxide of lead (litharge) and concentrated glycerine, unites wood to iron with remarkable efficiency. The composition is insoluble in most acids, is unaffected by the action of moderate heat, sets rapidly, and acquires an extraordinary hardness.

Marine Glue.—The true marine glue is a combination of shellac and caoutchouc in proportions which vary according to the purposes for which the cement is to be used. Some is very hard, others quite soft. The degree of softness is also regulated by the proportion of benzole used for dissolving the caoutchouc. Marine glue is more easily purchased than made, but where a small quantity is needed the following recipe is said to give very good results: Dissolve one part of

India-rubber in 12 parts of benzole, and to the solution add 20 parts of powdered shellac, heating the mixture cautiously over the fire. Apply with a brush.

The following recipe, taken from *New Remedies*, is said to yield a strong cement: 10 parts of caoutchouc or India-rubber are dissolved in 120 parts of benzine or petroleum (?) naphtha with the aid of a gentle heat. When the solution is complete, which sometimes requires 10 to 14 days, 20 parts of asphalt are melted in an iron vessel, and the caoutchouc solution is poured in very slowly, in a fine stream, and under continued heating, until the mass has become homogeneous, and nearly all of the solvent has been driven off. It is then poured out and cast into greased tin moulds. It forms dark-brown or black cakes, which are very hard to break. This cement requires considerable heat to melt it; and to prevent it from being burnt, it is best to heat a capsule containing a piece of it first on a water-bath, until the cake softens and begins to be liquid. It is then carefully wiped dry, and heated over a naked flame, under constant stirring, up to about 300° F. The edges of the article to be mended should, if possible, also be heated to at least 212° F., so as to permit the cement to be applied at leisure and with care. The thinner the cement is applied, the better it binds.

Metal, Cement for attaching to Glass.—Copal varnish, 15; drying oil, 5; turpentine, 3. Melt in a water-bath and add 10 parts slaked lime.

Paris Cement for mending Shells and other specimens.—Gum arabic, 5; sugar candy, 2. White lead, enough to color.

Paste.—The best paste is made of good flour, well boiled. Resin, etc., do more harm than good.

2. An excellent white paste may be made by dissolving 2½ oz. gum arabic in 2 quarts hot water and thickening with wheat flour. To this is added a solution of alum and sugar of lead; the mixture is heated and stirred till about to boil, when it is allowed to cool.

3. Four parts, by weight, of glue are allowed to soften in 15 parts of cold water for some hours, and then moderately heated till the solution becomes quite clear. 65 parts of boiling water are now added with stirring. In another vessel 30 parts of starch paste are stirred up with 20 parts of cold water, so that a thin milky fluid is obtained without lumps. Into this the boiling glue solution is poured, with constant

stirring, and the whole is kept at the boiling temperature. After cooling, 10 drops of carbolic acid are added to the paste. This paste is of extraordinary adhesive power, and may be used for leather, paper, or cardboard with great success. It must be preserved in closed bottles to prevent evaporation of the water, and will, in this way, keep good for years.

4. Rice flour makes an excellent paste for fine paper work.

5. Gum tragacanth and water make an ever ready paste. A few drops of any kind of acid should be added to the water before putting in the gum, to prevent fermentation. This paste will not give that semi-transparent look to thin paper, that gum arabic sometimes gives, when used for mucilage.

Porcelain Cement.—Add plaster of paris to a strong solution of alum till the mixture is of the consistency of cream. It sets readily, and is said to unite glass, metal, porcelain, etc., quite firmly. It is probably suited for cases in which large rather than small surfaces are to be united.

Soft Cement.—Melt yellow beeswax with its weight of turpentine and color with finely powdered venetian red. When cold it has the hardness of soap, but is easily softened and moulded with the fingers, and for sticking things together temporarily it is invaluable.

Soluble Glass Cements.—When finely-pulverized chalk is stirred into a solution of soluble glass of 30° B until the mixture is fine and plastic, a cement is obtained which will harden in between six and eight hours, possessing an extraordinary durability, and alike applicable for domestic and industrial purposes. If any of the following substances be employed besides chalk, differently-colored cements of the same general character are obtained:—1. Finely pulverized or levigated stibnite (grey antimony, or black sulphide of antimony) will produce a dark cement, which, after burnishing with an agate, will present a metallic appearance. 2. Pulverized cast iron, a grey cement. 3. Zinc dust (so-called zinc grey), an exceedingly hard grey cement, which, after burnishing, will exhibit the white and brilliant appearance of metallic zinc. This cement may be employed with advantage in mending ornaments and vessels of zinc, sticking alike well to metals, stone, and wood. 4. Carbonate of copper, a bright green cement. 5. Sesquioxide of chromium, a dark green cement. 6. Thénard's blue (cobalt blue), a blue cement.

7. Minium, an orange-colored cement. 8. Vermilion, splendid red cement. 9. Carmine red, a violet cement.

Sorel's Cement.—Mix commercial zinc white with ½ its bulk of fine sand, adding a solution of chloride of zinc of 1·26 specific gravity, and rub the whole thoroughly together in a mortar. The mixture must be applied at once, as it hardens very quickly.

Steam Boiler Cement.—Mix two parts of finely powdered litharge with one part of very fine sand, and one part of quicklime which has been allowed to slack spontaneously by exposure to the air. This mixture may be kept for any length of time without injuring. In using it a portion is mixed into paste with linseed oil, or, still better, boiled linseed oil. In this state it must be quickly applied, as it soon becomes hard.

Transparent Cement for Glass.—Fine Canada balsam.

Turner's Cement.—Melt 1 lb. of resin in a pan over the fire; and, when melted, add a ¼ of a lb. of pitch. While these are boiling add brick dust until, by dropping a little on a cold stone, you think it hard enough. In winter it may be necessary to add a little tallow. By means of this cement a piece of wood may be fastened to the chuck, which will hold when cool; and when the work is finished it may be removed by a smart stroke with the tool. Any traces of the cement may be removed from the work by means of benzine.

Wollaston's White Cement for large objects.—Beeswax, 1 oz.; resin, 4 oz.; powdered plaster of paris, 5 oz. Melt together. To use, warm the edges of the specimen and use the cement warm.

Copper.

Copper is probably the most difficult of all the metals to work by the file or lathe, but pure copper may be cut like cheese with a graver, and consequently it is extensively used for plates where the number of impressions required is not very large. In filing copper the file should be well chalked, and in cutting it in the lathe use plenty of soapy water, and let the solution of soap be pretty strong. In polishing copper it will be found that owing to its softness, it burnishes easily (see article on *polishing* metals), but where it is polished by means of abrasive processes, that is, by the use of powders which grind it or wear it down, great care must be taken to have the powders free from particles which are larger than the average, as these would be sure to scratch the metal, owing to its softness. For polishing copper by abrasion, only the softer polishing powders should be used, such as rotten stone, prepared chalk, and soft rouge. These are used with oil at first, but the last touches are given dry.

Copper may be welded by the use of proper fluxes. The best compound for this purpose is a mixture of one part of phosphate of soda and two parts of boracic acid. This welding powder should be strewn on the surface of the copper at a red heat; the pieces should then be heated up to a full cherry red, or yellow heat, and brought immediately under the hammer, when they may be as readily welded as iron itself. For instance, it is possible to weld together a small rod of copper which has been broken; the ends should be beveled, laid on one another, seized by a pair of tongs, and placed together with the latter in the fire and heated; the welding powder should then be strewn on the ends, which, after a further heating, may be welded so soundly as to bend and stretch as if they had never been broken. It is necessary to carefully observe two things in the course of the operation. First, the greatest care must be taken that no charcoal or other solid carbon comes into contact with the points to be welded, as otherwise phosphide of copper would be formed, which would cover the surface of the copper and effectually prevent a weld. In this case it is only by careful treatment in an oxidizing fire and a plentiful application of the welding powder that the copper can again be welded. It is, therefore, advisable to heat the copper in a flame, as, for instance, a gas flame. Second, as copper is a much softer metal than iron, it is much softer at the required heat than the latter at its welding heat, and the parts welded can not offer any great resistance to the blows of the hammer. They must, therefore, be so shaped as to be enabled to resist such blows as well as may be, and it is also well to use a wooden hammer, which does not exercise so great a force on account of its lightness. Mr. Rust, the inventor of this process, states that, as long ago as 1854, he welded strips of copper plates together and drew them into a rod; he also made a chain, the links of which had been made of pretty thick wire and welded.

Coppering Iron or Steel.—The following process is said to

give very good results: First make the article entirely bright by file, scratch brush, or any of the usual modes. Apply to the surface a coating of cream of tartar, then sprinkle the surface with a saturated solution of sulphate of copper, and rub with a hard brush. The coating of copper deposited on the iron is said to be very even and durable.

Coral, Artificial.

Twigs, raisin stalks, and any objects having the general outline of branched coral, may be made to resemble that material by being dipped in a mixture of 4 parts resin, 3 parts beeswax and 2 parts vermillion, melted together and thoroughly mixed. The effect is very pretty, and for ornamental work such imitation coral is very useful.

Cork.

Corks are so important in many operations, that a little knowledge of the best methods of working them is indispensable. They form the best material for a holder for sandpaper in rubbing down flat surfaces, and they afford the simplest and most effectual means of closing bottles in many cases. Cork is easily cut by means of a thin, sharp knife, which should not have a *smooth* edge, however, but one set on a dry stone, moderately fine. After having been cut to nearly the right form, corks are easily worked to the proper size and shape by means of files. Holes are easily made through corks by means of tin or brass tubes, which must be thin and well sharpened on the edge by means of a file. The sharp edge being slightly oiled, is pressed against the cork and at the same time turned round, when it quickly cuts a smooth straight hole through the material.

When it is desired to make corks air-tight and water-tight, the best method is to allow them to remain for about five minutes beneath the surface of melted paraffine in a suitable vessel, the corks being held down either by a perforated lid, wire screen, or similar device. Corks thus prepared can be easily cut and bored, have a perfectly smooth exterior, may be introduced and removed from the neck of a flask with ease, and make a perfect seal.

Crayons for Black-Boards.

Spanish white, which is simply very fine chalk, is mixed with water and just enough flour paste to cause the particles to adhere when dry. If too much paste is used, the crayons will be too hard and will not mark well; if too soft, they will crumble. The proper proportions should be found by experiment, as different qualities of flour possess different adhesive properties. The wet chalk may be formed into proper shape by means of paper moulds, or it may be rolled out to the required shape and cut into suitable lengths.

For making drawings of objects of natural history, etc., it is frequenely desirable to use colored crayons, the most useful colors being green, red and yellow. A little cheap, dry paint mixed with the chalk will give the desired tints.

Crayons which are not too hard to make a good clear mark, are very apt to be brittle and unable to stand any pressure on the point when they are of sufficient length to be handled easily. If the crayons are made true cylinders, they may be covered with paper, which will serve the same purpose as the wood in the common lead pencil, and may be cut away as wanted. The common crayons, being conical, are not so easily covered, but may, nevertheless, be wrapped with a long, narrow slip of paper so as to be strong and durable.

Curling.

A method of finishing such metals as brass, German silver, etc., which if well done, gives a very handsome appearance to the work. The work must first be carefully finished so as to have no scratches, as these would show through the curling and destroy the effect. After the metal has been finished with fine files, emery paper, Water-of-Ayr stone, and finally the finest rotten stone applied by means of a buff, the curling is produced by means of a stick of charcoal moved in circular sweeps over the surface, which should be kept well moistened with water. After the desired effect has been produced, the metal is lacquered.

We have seen "curling" applied to surfaces of considerable extent, but in such cases the effect never seemed to us as good as in the case of very small articles. If the sweeps are large they give a coarse appearance to the work, while a large surface covered with small sweeps has a confused appearance.

Cuticle, Liquid.

Collodion, or gun cotton dissolved in sulphuric ether, has no equal as a covering for protecting burns, cuts or wounds, from the air. It soon dries, and forms a skin-like protection that adheres with great tenacity.

Etching.

Etching is the art of cutting lines in any material by means of some corrosive agent. Thus, since nitric acid dissolves copper, if we confine the action of the acid to certain lines, we can cut grooves of considerable depth in the copper, and these grooves may be used either as lines from which we may print, or as marks similar to writing. Iron, brass, steel, silver, ivory, glass, marble, and many other materials may be cut in the same way, by the action of suitable acids. As a simple and easily learned method of forming engraved plates from which to print, the art of etching is one of the most eligible for young persons. The materials required are few and simple, great freedom of outline may be secured, and the results are very pleasing.

Copper is the metal usually employed for etching drawings. It is furnished by the dealers in plates perfectly smooth and flat, and of any desired size. The surface is first coated with a wax or varnish, for which there are many recipes, the following being probably the best: Take of beeswax and asphalt, 2 parts each; Burgundy pitch and black pitch, 1 part each. Melt the wax and the pitch in an earthen vessel and add the asphalt by degrees in fine powder. Expose to heat until a drop which has been cooled, breaks by bending back and forth two or three times in the fingers.

A second, which is simpler and said to be very good, is composed of asphalt, 2 oz.; Burgundy pitch, 1 oz.; beeswax, 1½ oz.

A transparent varnish may be composed of resin, 1 oz.; beeswax, 2 oz. Melt together.

The plate having been polished and burnished, is grasped by one corner in a hand-vice and warmed over a spirit lamp until it will melt the varnish or etching ground, which is then spread over its surface very thinly by means of a ball or pledget of cotton tied in a piece of silk. Before the ground has quite cooled and solidified, it is blackened by the smoke of a lamp or candle. The blackening is necessary so that the design may be clearly seen as it is drawn in.

The design may be either drawn directly on the plate, or transferred by means of transfer paper. Or it may be first drawn on the etching ground by means of a very finely pointed camel-hair pencil, using, of course, a white color dissolved in some medium which will adhere to the ground. Water is useless. Turpentine answers very well.

In whatever way the design is drawn on the surface of the ground, it must next be cut in by means of a steel point, good sewing needles making excellent ones, and different sizes being used according to the strength of the lines required. The lines having been traced through the varnish so as to expose a bright copper surface, the next step is to make a border of wax around the plate so that the acid will not run off. The wax used for making the border is a mixture of beeswax, resin and tallow, of such a consistency that it will be easily moulded by the fingers. The border should be nearly half an inch high, thus converting the plate into a shallow dish. This dish is half filled with a mixture of one part of nitric acid and three parts of water. After this plate has been exposed for a few minutes to this liquid, the acid is poured off, the plate washed with pure water and allowed to dry. All the very delicate lines are then "stopped" out, as it is called, by being coated by means of a camel-hair pencil with varnish dissolved in turpentine. When this has dried, the acid is poured back again and allowed to act on the coarser lines, and the more frequently this process is introduced, the more perfect will be the ultimate result.

When the lines have all been etched to the required depth, the varnish is removed by warming the plate and washing with turpentine. A copper-plate press is used to take off the impressions.

The process of etching is very simple, and the results very satisfactory. As an artistic recreation, it is capable of affording a great deal of pleasure.

The art of cutting names, etc., on steel tools and other objects, is very simple and useful. The following gives good results:

Etching Liquid for Steel.—Mix 1 oz. sulphate of copper, ¼ oz. of alum, and ½ a teaspoonful of salt reduced to powder, with 1 gill of vinegar and 20 drops of nitric acid. This liquid may be used either for eating deeply into the metal or for imparting a beautiful frosted appearance to the surface, according to the time it is allowed to act. Cover the parts you wish to protect from its influence with beeswax, tallow, or some similar substance.

Etching on Glass.—Fancy work, ornamental figures, lettering and monograms, are most easily and neatly cut into glass by the sand blast process, a simple apparatus for which will be found described in the *Young Scientist*. Lines and figures on tubes, jars, etc., may be deeply etched by smearing the surface of the glass with beeswax, drawing the lines with a steel point, and exposing the glass to the fumes of hydrofluoric acid. This acid is obtained by putting powdered fluorspar into a tray made of sheet lead and pouring sulphuric acid on it, after which the tray is slightly warmed.

The proportions will, of course, vary with the purity of the materials used, fluorspar (except when in crystals) being generally mixed with a large quantity of other matter, but this point need not affect the success of the operation. Enough acid to make a thin paste with the powdered spar will be about right. Where a lead tray is not at hand, the powdered spar may be poured on the glass, and the acid poured on it and left for some time. As a general rule, the marks are opaque, but sometimes they are transparent. In this case, cut them deeply and fill up with black varnish, if they are required to be very plain, as in the case of graduated vessels.

Liquid hydrofluoric acid has been recommended for etching, but as it leaves the surface on which it acts *transparent*, it is not suitable.

The agent which corrodes the glass is a gas which does not *remain* in the mixture of fluorspar and sulphuric acid, but passes off in the vapor. To mix fluorspar and sulphuric acid and keep it in leaden bottles under the idea that the mixture is *hydrofluoric acid*, is a gross mistake. Such an idea could enter into the head of none but the compiler of a cyclopaedia of recipes.

Eye, Accidents to.

Those who are engaged in mechanical operations run great risk of accidents to the eye, and therefore a few hints in regard to this subject may be valuable to our readers.

Minute particles of dust, sand, cinders, small flies, etc., are best removed by means of a camel-hair brush or pencil, moistened but not wet, and drawn to a fine point. The brush will absorb the moisture of the eye and with it will take up the mote, provided the latter has not been driven into the eyeball. Where a brush is not at hand, a thin strip of soft paper, rolled spirally so as to form a fine point, is the best thing.

The ragged chips and splinters which are separated during the processes of turning and chipping off, often find their way into the eye, and are sometimes very difficult to remove. The use of magnets has been recommended, but even the strongest magnet is entirely inefficient, if the splinters be imbedded. In such a case, if the operator be gifted with a steady hand and firm nerves, the best instrument for removing the offending particle is a good, sharp pen-knife. Indeed, we prefer it in every case as being far superior to softer articles. In simple cases let the patient stand up with his head firmly held against a door-post; turn back the eyelids with the fingers; find the speck, and by passing the knife gently but firmly over the ball, you may sweep it up. Where the splinter is actually imbedded in the eye, lay the patient on his back on a table; turn the eyelids back, and fix them by means of a ring, and then you will find yourself free to operate without danger of interference from the patient's winking. A suitable ring may be found in most bunches of keys, or any mechanic can make one in two minutes out of a piece of stiff iron wire. Iron splinters always have ragged edges, and can be caught on the fine, sharp edge of a knife and lifted out. But although we recommend the use of a sharp knife, it must be remembered that no cutting of the eyeball is to be permitted in any case, except by an experienced oculist.

Where the person who is operating is at all nervous or timid, it will not do to use a knife. In this case, take some soft, white silk waste and wind it round a splinter of wood so as to completely cover the end and form a little brush of looped threads. Tie it fast. When such a brush is swept over that part of the eyeball where the offending substance is imbedded, the latter will soon be entangled in the threads and may be easily drawn out.

In all such cases a good magnifier will be found of great assistance. The best form is perhaps a good watchmaker's glass.

When corrosive chemicals, such as oil of vitriol, nitric acid, corrosive salts, etc., find their way into the eye, the best application is abundance of pure cold water. The eye should be *held* open and well washed out. When any irritating substance gets into the eye, the lid is apt to close spasmodically, and if allowed to remain so, no water can get in.

In the case of lime, however, the action of water would only increase the difficulty. A little vinegar and water forms the best wash for lime, potash, soda, or ammonia.

Fires.

Most of the fires that occur might be avoided by proper care, and the following hints, if carefully observed, will aid materially in avoiding such accidents:

1. Never leave matches where they can be reached by children, and if one should fall on the floor, be careful and search for it until you find it. A match, when trodden on, readily ignites, and if unobserved may cause a serious fire, or what is more likely, set a lady's dress in flames. Rats and mice have a great fondness for matches, and often carry them off to their holes, where, by nibbling, they set them on fire. Always keep matches in tin boxes, and never in paper packages.

2. Children should be strictly prevented from playing with fire, and severely punished if caught so offending. It is far better that they should undergo the inconvenience of a little wholesome chastisement than either set the house on fire, disfigure themselves for life, or be burnt to death, from the want of being severely punished for disobedience.

3. Never leave a lamp or candle burning at your bedside on a table when you go to bed, and avoid reading in bed; this is a most fruitful cause of loss of life and property.

4. If a piece of paper is used to light a lamp, see that it is properly extinguished before leaving it, as it will sometimes burst out on fire after it is supposed to have been completely extinguished.

5. If there be an escape of gas, so that the smell of it is very apparent, open the door and windows immediately to allow its escape, and facilitate the entrance of fresh air; and above all things avoid coming any way near with a light of any description. As soon as you can, shut off the gas at the meter.

6. Be careful about stove-pipes passing through lath partitions; about kindling wood left in the oven over night to dry, and about the ash-box. Never keep ashes in a wooden vessel under any circumstances whatever, and never go to

bed at night without seeing that every possible cause for an accidental fire has been removed. Allow no linen or cotton clothes to hang near a stove over night for the purpose of drying them.

7. There never yet was a fire which a single pail of water, if applied in time, would not have quenched, therefore never go to bed without having a few pails of water at hand, and a dipper with which to throw it on the fire. Water can never be so well applied if thrown from the pail itself. Spontaneous combustion is no imaginary danger, therefore never leave heaps of oiled rags and similar rubbish lying around.

As most of us are liable to be caught in a burning building, it would be well for us to impress the following hints upon the mind, as they may stand us in good stead if a fire should occur:

1. Every householder should make each person in his house acquainted with the best means of escape, whether the fire breaks out at the top or at the bottom. In securing the street door and lower windows for the night, avoid complicated fastenings or impediments to an immediate outlet in case of fire.

2. Inmates, at the first alarm, should endeavor to reflect what means of escape there are in the house; if in bed at the time, wrap themselves in a blanket or bedside carpet; open neither windows nor doors more than necessary; shut every door after them. This is most important to observe.

3. In the midst of smoke it is comparatively clear toward the ground, consequently progress through the smoke can be made on the hands and knees. A silk handkerchief, worsted stockings, or other flannel substance wetted and drawn over the face, permits free breathing, and excludes, to a great extent, the smoke from the lungs. A wet sponge is alike efficacious.

4. In the event of being unable to escape, either by the street door or roof, the persons in danger should immediately make their way to a front room window, taking care to close the door after them, and those who have charge of the household should ascertain that every individual is there assembled.

5. Persons thus circumstanced should never precipitate themselves from the windows while there remains the least probability of assistance; and even in the last extremity a plain rope is invaluable, or recourse may be had to joining

sheets or blankets together, fastening one end round the bedpost or other furniture. This will enable one person to lower all the others separately, and the last may let himself down with comparatively little risk. Select a window over the doorway rather than over the area.

Clothes on Fire.—So many accidents are daily occurring from broken kerosene lamps, and clothes taking fire from gas lights and open fire-places, that it is very important to know what to do under such circumstances. Three persons out of four would rush right up to the burning individual, and begin to paw with their hands without any aim. It is useless to tell the victim to do this or that, or call for water. In fact it is generally best not to say a word, but seize a blanket from a bed, or a cloak, or any woolen fabric—if none is at hand, take any heavy material—hold the corners as far apart as you can, stretch them higher than your head, and running boldly to the person, make a motion of clasping in the arms, just about the shoulders. This instantly smothers the fire and saves the face. The next instant throw the unfortunate person on the floor. This is an additional safety to the face and breath, and any remnant of flame can be put out more leisurely. When the person whose clothes take fire is alone, the danger is not unfrequently increased by the sufferer running about in a state of alarm; whereas it would be better for him to roll on the floor until the fire is extinguished, or better still, to cover himself with a loose carpet, rug, or blanket, to exclude the air, till a sufficient supply of water is obtained to throw over him. In either case, after the fire has been put out, the individual should be placed on a bed, and the clothes removed piecemeal by cutting them off; much caution is required in taking away the body linen without tearing off the skin, and where the linen sticks, so much only should be cut off as can be detached readily.

Fire Proof Dresses.—Some years ago Queen Victoria appointed a commission to investigate this subject. It was found that there were but four salts which were applicable to light fabrics: 1, Phosphate of ammonia; 2, a mixture of phosphate of ammonia and chloride of ammonia; 3, sulphate of ammonia; 4, tungstate of soda. Of these, the best was tungstate of soda, a salt which is not by any means expensive. Sulphate of ammonia is objectionable, from the fact that it acts on the irons and moulds the fabric. The tungstate of soda is neither injurious to the texture or color, or in any degree difficult of application in the washing process. The iron passes over the material quite as smoothly as if no solution had been employed. The solution increases the stiffness of the fabric, and its protecting power against fire is perfect. This salt offers only one difficulty, viz: the formation of a bitungstate, of little solubility, which crystallizes from the solution; but it was found that a very small percentage of phosphate of soda rendered the tungstate quite stable. The best method of applying these salts is to take one ounce of tungstate of soda and a quarter of an ounce of phosphate of soda, and dissolve them in a quart of water. The goods are moistened with this solution before being starched, and they may be afterwards ironed and finished without the least difficulty.

Articles prepared in this way are perfectly uninflammable. They may be charred by exposure to fire, but they do not burn readily unless there is some extraneous source of heat, and they can not be made to burst into flame. By the aid of this discovery, a lady dressed in the lightest muslin might walk over a row of footlights, and the only result would be that the lower part of her dress would be injured. Unless her person actually came in contact with the gas flames, she herself would suffer no injury. In country places, where tungstate of soda cannot be procured, a mixture of three parts borax, and two and a half parts sulphate of magnesia, in twenty parts of water, may be used with good effect.

Fly-Papers.

Sticky or adhesive fly-papers are to be discouraged, as it is a cruelty to subject even flies to the long struggles and slow death caused by it. Such papers, however, are occasionally sold, and are prepared by coating paper with factitious bird-lime. Or the bird-lime is smeared upon wooden sticks standing in a base, for instance, a flower-pot, when they will adhere to it. A better plan is to mix some poison with the adhesive mass, but care should be taken lest children get at it. Cooley gives the following formula: Treacle, honey, or moist sugar mixed with about 1-12th of their weight of orpiment (yellow tersulphide of arsenic). Redwood's formula is: Small quassia chips, ¼ oz.; water, 1 pint; boil 10 minutes, strain, and add 4 oz. of treacle. Flies will drink this with avidity, and are soon destroyed by it.

Freezing Mixtures.

The temperatures here given are Fahrenheit. When ice or snow are not to be had and it is desired to cool any solid, liquid or gas, a good freezing mixture is the simplest method of accomplishing the object. The following mixtures are the most convenient and efficient:

1. Nitrate of ammonia, carbonate of soda and water, equal parts by weight. The thermometer sinks 57°.

2. Phosphate of soda, 9 parts; nitrate of ammonia, 6 parts; diluted nitric acid, (acid 1 part, water 2 parts,) 4 parts. Reduces the temperature 71° or from 50° to — 21°.

3. Sal ammoniac, 5 parts; nitrate of potash, 5 parts; sulphate of soda, 8 parts; water, 16 parts. Reduces the temperature 46° or from 70° to 24°. This is one of the cheapest, most readily procured, and most convenient of mixtures.

Freezing mixtures are often used when it is required to produce a greater degree of cold than can be obtained by the mere application of ice. When ice is at hand, as it generally is in this country, the following should be used:

1. Finely pounded ice, 2 parts; salt, 1 part. This mixture reduces the temperature to 5°.

2. Finely pounded ice, 2 parts; crystallized chloride of calcium, 3 parts. Reduces the temperature from 32° to — 40°.

3. Finely pounded ice, 7 parts; diluted nitric acid, 4 parts. Reduces the temperature from 32° to — 30°.

In every case the materials should be kept as cool as possible. Thus the ice should be pounded in a cooled mortar with a cooled pestle, and the mixture should be made in vessels previously cooled. By attention to these particulars it is easy to freeze mercury at any time by means of these simple and easily practiced methods, though, of course, the modern laboratory is provided with agencies of far greater cooling power.

Fumigating Pastils.

For the purpose of deodorizing a room in which there is an offensive smell, common coffee berries, and even rags or brown paper, if properly burned, will serve admirably. The smoke from these substances not only neutralizes the odors, but really acts as a disinfectant to a slight extent. In burning coffee, paper or rags for this purpose, care must be taken to prevent them from burning too freely. If they burn with a free, bright flame, the proper effect will not be produced. They should be allowed to smoulder quietly, and they do this best when they are thrown on hot coals, or a hot shovel and set on fire.

An excellent substitute for pastils is heavy brown paper, which has been dipped in a solution of nitre and then dried. This burns freely without flame, and if it be dipped in a solution of benzoin, the odor is very pleasant. The best thing, however, is pastils. They are easily made as follows:

1. *Paris Formula.*—Benzoin, 2 oz.; balsam of tolu and yellow sandal wood, of each 4 drachms; nitre, 2 drachms; labdanum, 1 drachm; charcoal, 6 oz. Reduce to powder, mix thoroughly and make into a stiff paste with gum tragacanth. Form into small cones and dry them in the air.

2. *Formula of Henry and Guibourt.*—Powdered benzoin, 16 parts; balsam of tolu and powdered sandal wood, each 4 parts; charcoal powder, 48 parts; powdered tragacanth and labdanum, each 1 part; powdered nitre and gum arabic, each 2 parts; make into a paste with 12 parts cinnamon water, form into cones and dry.

3. The following formula is somewhat complex, but gives very fine results: Take the charcoal of any light wood, 200 parts; gum benzoin, 100 parts; powdered sandal wood, 50 parts; balsam of tolu, 50 parts; Storax (Styrax calamita), 50 parts; gum olibanum, 50 parts; cascarilla bark, 100 parts; cloves, 40 parts; cinnamon (Ceylon), 40 parts; potassium nitrate, 75 parts. Reduce the ingredients to powder, and mix them with oil of Ceylon cinnamon, 5 parts; oil of cloves, 5 parts; oil of lavender, 5 parts; balsam of Peru, 10 parts; camphor, powdered, 1 part. Then add mucilage of tragacanth sufficient to make a mass which is to be formed into conical cylinders about ¾ to 1 inch high, and ending at the bottom in three projections. Dry them in a warm place.

Gilding.

A covering of gold, when judiciously applied to the proper parts of any object adds greatly to its beauty, and in the case of metals, such as steel, copper, silver, etc., the gold, being capable of resisting the action of most chemical agents, proves a very perfect protector against corrosion. Metals are now generally gilt by means of the electrotype process, though the old method by means of an amalgam, is still used in some cases. Stamped goods, such as cheap jewelry, are also made out of sheets of metal which, after being heavily gilt, are rolled out thin, the gold being thus spread over an astonishing extent of surface. For gilding leather, wood, etc., gold in the form of leaf or powder is generally used.

Gilding with Gold-Leaf.—There are various methods applicable, according to the different circumstances and the character of the objects to be gilded. Book-binders use gold-leaf in two ways—to gild on the edge, and to place gold letters on the binding. To gild on the edge, the edge is smoothly cut, put in a strong press, scraped so as to make it solid, and the well-beaten white of an egg or albumen put on thinly; the gold-leaf is then put on before the albumen is dry; it is pressed down with cotton, and when dry polished with an agate polisher. To put on the lettering, the place where the letters are to appear is coated with albumen, and after it is dry, the type to be used is heated to about the boiling point of water, the gold-leaf put on, either on the book or on the type, and then placed on the spot where the lettering is desired, when the gold-leaf will adhere by the heat of the type, while the excess of gold-leaf loosely around is rubbed off with a tuft of cotton.

To do printing with gold-leaf, the sheet to be printed on is pinned to the tympan of a hand-press, and it is first printed with ink of any color, or with varnish, and then the type is covered with a large sheet of paper, the gold-leaf laid on, and the tympan laid down again, slowly and carefully, so as not to disturb the gold-leaf by motions of the air; then the pressure is again applied, when the gold-leaf will stick to the printed sheet, and the surplus can be rubbed off with a tuft of cotton. Ordinary printing in gold, silver and bronze, however, is done with powdered metal and not with leaf. The printing is first done with a varnish specially made for the purpose; after the impression has been taken, the sheets are allowed to lie a short time so as to dry a little, but not completely, and while still *tacky* the gold, silver or bronze powder is sprinkled over the letters. The powder adheres to the varnish, and the surplus is easily removed by means of a tuft of cotton.

In gilding picture-frames with gold-leaf there are two methods; one with the ordinary gold size, the other with **varnish**. The latter method does not allow polishing, but is water-proof; the former is not. The main point is to have a well prepared ground-work of say white lead and drying oil, smoothed down properly; then follow several coats of calcined white lead in linseed oil and turpentine, with intervals of at least twenty-four hours between each coat, which must be carefully smoothed off with pumice-stone and fine emery-paper. Then the gold size is applied, which may be made from the sediment that collects at the bottom of the pot in which painters wash their brushes; this is thoroughly ground and strained. When the gold size coat is sufficiently dry so as to be a little sticky, apply the gold-leaf and press it on with cotton or a soft brush; after a few days' hardening it is varnished with spirits or oil varnish. This gives a water-proof gilding, but ordinarily picture-frames are gilded with a gold size containing no oil. It is made of finely ground sal ammoniac, to which is added a very little beef suet; this is mixed with a pallet-knife, with parchment size dissolved in water, so as to flow from the knife when hot. The frame may be prepared first with a few coats of Paris white and glue-water, rubbed down smoothly, and finally apply the size, which must not be too thick, as then it will chip off, and if too thin it will not have sufficient body. The most difficult part in all these operations of gold-leaf gilding, is the application of the gold-leaf, which requires much practice, judgment, and great care, but with some attention to little details it can be easily learned. There ought to be no draught at the place of operation and the operator ought to avoid allowing his breath to blow upon the gold leaves, as they are so thin and light that the least breath of air causes them to fly about—worse than feathers. Turn the gold leaves—one at a time—out of the book upon the leather cushion; with the gilding-knife you may lift any leaf and carry it to a convenient place to cut it into the sizes required. Blow gently on the center of the leaf, and it will at once spread out and lie flat without any wrinkles, then cut it by passing the edge of the knife over it until divided. Place the work to be gilded as near as practicable in a horizontal position, and with a long camels'-hair pencil, dipped in a mixture of water with a little brandy, go over as much surface as the piece of gold is to cover; then take up the gold from the cushion with a tip. Drawing it over the forehead and cheek will dampen it sufficiently to make the gold adhere. This must then be carefully transferred to its place on the work, and by gently breathing on it, it will adhere. Take care that the part to which it is applied be sufficiently wet, so that the gold-leaf will not crack. Proceed in this way, a little at a time, not attempting to cover too much at once. If any cracks or flaws appear, immediately apply another piece of gold-leaf over it—large enough to cover the crack. If occasionally the gold does not appear to adhere, on account of the ground having become too dry, run a wet pencil close to the edge of the gold, so as to allow water to penetrate under the gold-leaf. When the work is dry (say in ten or twelve hours), it may be burnished with an agate tool, taking care to first remove all the dust from the tool as well as from the gilded surface.

Ornamental lines of gilding may be painted on wood and other articles by means of a fine camel-hair brush, using shell gold, which may be had at the artists' supply stores. This forms a very good method of ornamenting work done by the scroll saw, or carved work, such as frames, etc.

Gilding Steel.—Polished steel may be beautifully gilded by means of the ethereal solution of gold. Dissolve pure gold in aqua regia, evaporate gently to dryness, so as to drive off the superfluous acid, re-dissolve in water and add three times its bulk of sulphuric ether. Allow to stand for twenty-four hours in a stoppered bottle and the ethereal solution of gold will float at top. Polished steel dipped in this is at once beautifully gilded, and by tracing patterns on the surface of the metal with any kind of varnish, beautiful devices in plain metal and gilt will be produced. For other metals the electro process is the best.

Glass Working.

Glass is usually brought into shape by being moulded or blown. Simple and complete directions for blowing small articles may be found in the *Young Scientist*, vol. I, p. 37.

There are a few other operations, however, which are constantly needed by the amateur and which we will describe.

Cutting Glass.—For cutting flat glass, such as window-panes, and for cutting rounds or ovals out of flat glass, the diamond is the best tool; and, if the operator has no diamond it will always pay to carry the job to a glazier rather than waste time and make a poor job by other and inferior means. When, however, it is required to cut off a very little from a circle or oval, the diamond is not available, except in very skilful hands. In this case a pair of pliers softened by heating, or very dull scissors is the best tool, and the cutting is best performed under water. A little practice will enable the operator to shape a small round or oval with great rapidity, ease and precision. When bottles or flasks are to be cut, the diamond is still the best tool in skilful hands; but ordinary operators will succeed best with pastils, or a red hot poker with a pointed end. We prefer the latter, as being the most easily obtained and the most efficient; and we have never found any difficulty in cutting off broken flasks so as to make dishes, or to carry a cut spirally round a long bottle so as to cut it into the form of a corkscrew. And, by the way, when so cut, glass exhibits considerable elasticity, and the spiral may be elongated like a ringlet. The process is very simple. The line of the cut should be marked by chalk or by pasting a thin strip of paper alongside of it; then make a file mark to commence the cut; apply the hot iron and a crack will start; and this crack will follow the iron wherever we choose to lead it. In this way jars are easily made out of old bottles, and broken vessels of different kinds may be cut up into new forms. Flat glass may also be cut into the most intricate and elegant forms. The red hot iron is far superior to strings wet with turpentine, friction, etc.

Drilling Glass.—For drilling holes in glass, a common steel drill, well made and well tempered, is the best tool. The steel should be forged at a low temperature, so as to be sure not to burn it, and then tempered as hard as possible in a bath of salt water that has been well boiled. Such a drill will go through glass very rapidly if kept well moistened with turpentine in which some camphor has been dissolved. Dilute sulphuric acid is equally good, if not better. It is stated, that at Berlin, glass castings for pump-barrels, etc., are drilled, planed and bored, like iron ones, and in the same lathes and machines, by the aid of sulphuric acid. A little practice with these different plans will enable the operator to cut and work glass as easily as brass or iron.

Turning Glass in the Lathe.—Black diamonds are now so easily procured that they are the best tools for turning, planing or boring glass where much work is to be done. With a good diamond a skilful worker can turn a lens roughly out of a piece of flat glass in a few seconds, so that it will be very near the right shape.

A splinter of diamond may be very readily fastened in the end of a piece of stout brass wire so that it may be used for drilling or turning glass. Bore a hole the size of the splinter and so deep that the diamond may be inserted beyond its largest part, but leaving the point projecting. Then, by means of a pair of stout pliers, it is easy to press the end of the brass so that it will fill in around the diamond and hold it tight. Diamonds are sometimes cemented in such holes by means of shellac, or even solder run around them. This answers for some purposes, but not for drilling or turning.

Fitting Glass Stoppers.—Very few stoppers fit properly the bottles for which they are intended. The stoppers and bottles are ground with copper cones, fed with sand and made to revolve rapidly in a lathe, and the common stock are not specially fitted. To fit a stopper to a bottle that has not been ground, use emery or coarse sand kept constantly wet with water, and replaced with fresh as fast as it is reduced to powder. When all the surface has become equally rough, it is considered a sign that the glass has been ground to the proper shape, as until that time the projecting parts only show traces of erosion. This is the longest and hardest part of the work, as after that the glass simply needs finishing and polishing. For that purpose emery only can be used, owing to the fact that the material can be obtained of any degree of fineness, in this respect differing from sand. Otherwise the operation is the same as before, the emery being always kept moistened, and replaced when worn out. The grinding is continued until both the neck of the bottle and the stopper acquire a uniform finish, of a moderate degree of smoothness, and until the stopper fits so accurately that no shake can be felt in it, even though it be not twisted in tightly.

Glass Stoppers.—To remove glass stoppers when tightly fixed, it has been recommended to apply a cloth wet in hot water. This is an inconvenient and frequently unsuccessful method. The great object is to expand the neck of the bottle so as to loosen it on the stopper. If, however, the latter be heated and expanded equally with the former, the desired effect is not produced; and this is often the case in applying hot water. By holding the neck of the bottle about half an inch above the flame of a lamp or candle, for a few seconds, we have never failed in the most obstinate cases. The hands should be wrapped in a towel, and great care should be taken not to let the flame touch the glass, as this might cause it to crack. The bottle should be kept rapidly turning, during the operation, so as to bring all parts of the neck equally under the influence of the heat, when it will be rapidly expanded and the stopper may be withdrawn by a *steady* pull and twist. Sometimes it is necessary to tap the stopper lightly with a piece of wood; the jar is very apt to loosen the stopper. To twist the stopper, make, in a piece of wood, an oblong hole into which the stopper will just fit.

Glass, To Powder.—Powdered glass is frequently used instead of paper, cloth, cotton or sand for filtering varnishes, acids, etc. It is not soluble or corrodible. Sand, if purely silicious, would be better, but such sand is difficult to get; it too often contains matters which are easily corroded or dissolved. Powdered glass when glued to paper is also used for polishing wood and other materials. It cuts rapidly and cleanly, and is better than sand for most purposes. Glass is easily pulverized after being heated red hot and plunged into cold water. It cracks in every direction, becomes hard and brittle, and breaks with keenly cutting edges. After being pounded in a mortar it may be divided into powders of different degrees of fineness by being sifted through lawn sieves.

Glass, Imitation Ground—Put a piece of putty in muslin, twist the fabric tight, and tie it into the shape of a pad; well clean the glass first, and then putty it all over. The putty will exude sufficiently through the muslin to render the stain opaque. Let it dry hard, and then varnish. If a pattern is required, cut it out in paper as a stencil; place it so as not to slip, and proceed as above, removing the stencil when finished. If there should be any objection to the existence of the clear spaces, cover with slightly opaque varnish. In this way very neat and cheap signs may be painted on glass doors.

Glass Ware, Packing.—Every one has this duty to perform occasionally, and it is well to know how it should be done. The safety of glass articles packed together in a box does not depend so much upon the quantity of packing material used, as upon the fact that no two pieces of glass come into actual contact. In packing plates, a single straw placed between two of them will prevent them from breaking each other. In packing bottles in a case, such as the collecting case of the microscopist, and the test case of the chemist, rubber rings slipped over each, will be found the best and handiest packing material. They have this great advantage that they do not give rise to dust.

Washing Glass Vessels.—In many operations where glass vessels are used, success will depend upon having the glass perfectly clean. Upon this subject a correspondent of the *Chemical News* says: Such a subject may seem too simple, but yet the more I see students at their work, the more I am impressed with the fact that but few know how to wash a beaker-glass clean. Some time since I took beakers from various students in my laboratory (which they had washed and put away), and held them under a powerful stream of water until they were thoroughly wet. On taking them from under the spout, in almost every case the water ran off the glass in spots, showing that the glass was greasy. The best thing to wash beakers, etc., with, according to my experience, is sand-soap. Naturally, the sand must not be sharp. The soaps containing infusorial earth are most excellent for this purpose. Borax soap is also very efficacious. A piece of board about 20 cm. long, 15 cm. wide, and 4 cm. thick, should be screwed on to the right (inside) of the sink. In this block a rectangular hole, about 2 cm. deep and 1 cm. smaller than the section of the soap when stood on its long end, is to be cut. The bottom of the cake of soap is then whittled away so that it fits tightly in the hole. It is now moistened and pushed into the aperture, where it remains tightly fixed. By wetting the right hand thoroughly, and rubbing on this soap ridge, a good lather is made. With the soapy hand the glass is rubbed and washed until, on taking it from under the stream, no oily spots appear, the glass appearing wet all over. The beaker is then dried with a good towel ("glass towel"), and finally polished with a piece of chamois or kid leather. The final polish with kid is necessary, since the best towel leaves fibres on the glass. In cleaning test tubes, it is only necessary to rub the probang on the soap.

For cleaning flasks and bottles which have been soiled with varnishes or resins, or for cleaning the glass slides used for microscopic objects, proceed as follows: Remove all the balsam, resin, varnish, etc., possible by means of heat, scraping, and a solution of soda or potash. When the article is as clean as possible, place it in strong sulphuric acid, to which must be added as much powdered bichromate of potassa.

The chromic acid will quickly destroy all organic matter, and the article when washed in pure water will be found perfectly clean.

Grass.

Grass, To Stain Dried.—There are few prettier ornaments, and none more economical and lasting, than bouquets of dried grasses mingled with the various unchangeable flowers. They have but one fault, and that is this, the want of other colors besides yellow and drab or brown. To vary their shade artificially, these flowers are sometimes dyed green. This, however, is in bad taste and unnatural. The best effect is produced by blending rose and red tints together, and with a very little pale blue with the grasses and flowers as they dry naturally. The best means of dyeing dried leaves, flowers and grasses, is to dip them into the alcoholic solution of the various compounds of aniline. Some of these have a beautiful rose shade; others red, blue, orange and purple. The depth of color can be regulated by diluting, if necessary, the original dyes, with alcohol, down to the shade desired. When taken out of the dye, they should be exposed to the air to dry off the alcohol. They then require arranging or setting into form, as, when wet, the petals and fine filaments have a tendency to cling together. A pink saucer, as sold by most druggists, will supply enough rose dye for two ordinary bouquets. The pink saucer yields the best rose dye by washing it off with water and lemon juice. The aniline dyes yield the best violet, mauve and purple colors.

Guns.

The excellence of a gun depends very much upon the form and finish of the interior of the barrels, and as the owner may, if he chooses, work the inside of his gun over so as to improve it, we give a few directions.

Freeing.—It has been found that a perfect cylindrical tube is not the best form for a gun barrel. Guns shoot most closely and strongly when the bore is *very slightly* enlarged towards the muzzle. This enlargement is easily effected by means of very fine emery paper wrapped about a round rod and used with a little oil. The freeing may extend to about one-third of the length of the barrel, and the gun should be tested from time to time during the process, so as to get the very best results. The testing is done by firing a standard charge of powder and shot at a sheet of brown paper and noting the number of pellets that are put into a circle of given size, and also the force with which they are driven into a board. For ordinary bird guns, a 30-inch circle at forty yards, makes a good target.

To Keep Barrels from Rusting.—One of the great difficulties which the sportsman has to contend against is the rusting of his barrels, even when protected by the best browning. The alkaline matter existing in snow and in rain, under certain conditions of the atmosphere, works through the best coatings, and reaches the iron. Varnish, as ordinarily laid on, is objectionable, as it gives a gun a "Brummagem" look. The best plan is the following: Heat the barrels to the temperature of boiling water (not any hotter, or you may injure them), and rub them with the best copal varnish, giving them a plentiful coating. Let them remain hot for half an hour, and then wipe them clean with a soft rag. In this way you can get enough of the varnish into the pores of the metal to act as a preservative, and, at the same time, no one would suspect that the barrels had ever been touched with varnish. We have applied boiled oil, beeswax, paraffin, and some other substances, in the same way, and obtained good results; but on the whole, we find nothing better than good copal varnish.

Browning Gun Barrels.—To obtain a handsomely browned barrel, we must not only use a first rate recipe, but we must apply a good deal of skill and no small amount of hard work. When barrels are imperfectly browned, the fault lies more frequently in defective work than in the use of a poor recipe. The following are the directions given in the United States Ordnance Manual, and it is to be presumed that these are the directions that are followed in the government armories.

Materials for Browning Mixture.—Spirits of wine, 1½ oz.; tincture of steel, 1½ oz.; corrosive sublimate, 1½ oz.; sweet spirits of nitre, 1½ oz.; blue vitriol, 1 oz.; nitric acid, ¾ oz. To be mixed and dissolved in one quart of warm water, the mixture to be kept in glass bottles and not in earthen jugs.

Previous to commencing the operation of browning, it is necessary that the barrel or other part should be made quite bright with emery or a fine smooth file (but not burnished), after which it must be carefully cleaned from all greasiness; a small quantity of powdered lime rubbed well over every part of the barrel, is the best for this purpose, but in the case of old work, which is very oily or greasy, or when the oil or grease has become dried or gummed on the surface, the barrels must be first washed with a strong solution of potash in warm water. After this the lime may be applied. Plugs of wood are then to be put into the muzzle of the barrel and into the vent, and the mixture applied to every part with a clean sponge or rag. The barrel is then to be exposed to the air for twenty-four hours, after which time it is to be well rubbed over with a steel *scratch-card* or *scratch-brush*, until the rust is entirely removed; the mixture may then be applied again, as before, and in a few hours the barrel will be sufficiently corroded for the operation of scratch-brushing to be repeated. The same process of scratching off the rust and applying the mixture is to be repeated twice or three times a day for four or five days, by which time the barrel will be of a very dark brown color.

When the barrel is sufficiently brown, and the rust has been carefully removed from every part, about a quart of boiling water should be poured over every part of the barrel, in order that the action of the acid mixture upon the barrel may be destroyed, and the rust thereby prevented from rising again.

The barrel, when cold, should afterwards be rubbed over with linseed oil or sperm oil. It is particularly directed that the steel scratch-card or scratch-brush be used in the place of a hard hair-brush, otherwise the browning will not be durable nor have a good appearance.

If the work be handled with unclean or greasy hands, imperfectly browned places will show where the hands have touched the barrels.

Varnish for Browned Iron.—Shellac, 1 oz.; dragon's blood, 3-16ths of an oz.; alcohol, 1 quart.

Very complete directions for browning gun-barrels may be found in a little book called "Shooting on the Wing," which may be obtained from the publishers of this volume.

Handles, To Fasten.

The handles of knives, forks, and similar articles, that have come off by being put in hot water, may be fastened on in the following manner:

1. Take powdered resin and mix with it a small quantity of powdered chalk, whiting or slaked lime. Fill the hole in the handle with the mixture, heat the tang of the knife or fork and thrust in. When cold it will be securely fastened.

2. Take one lb. resin and 8 oz. sulphur, melt together, form into bars, or when cold reduce to powder. One part of the powder is to be mixed with half a part of iron filings, brick dust or fine sand; fill the cavity of the handle with the mixture and insert the tang, previously heated.

3. Brick dust and powdered resin, make a very good composition. It may be melted and poured into the handle, or powdered and then put in, and the tang inserted warm.

4. Chopped hair, flax, hemp or tow, mixed with powdered resin and applied as above.

5. One pound colophony, 8 oz. sulphur; melt, and when cool reduce to powder. Mix with this some fine sand or brick dust, and use as stated.

6. Take a portion of a quill, put it into the handle, warm the tang and insert it into the quill in the handle, and press it firmly. This is a simple method, and answers the purpose required very well.

Ink.

The varieties of writing-fluids that have been devised and introduced are almost innumerable, but for practical purposes the inks in common use may be divided into three classes, viz: 1. Those which consist of a powder mechanically divided and suspended in water by means of mucilage. 2. Those which consist of chemical precipitates held in suspension in the same way. 3. Those which consist of a true solution of some coloring matter, such as aniline or carmine. Of the first class, Indian or China ink is the great type. It consists of carbon in the form of very fine lamp-black, ground to a state of impalpable fineness in water, and mixed with some pure form of gelatine. Its use is wholly restricted to draughtsmen, who prefer it for several reasons. In the first place, it gives the finest and clearest black of any ink known; second, it is unchangeable; and in the third place, it does not corrode the fine and expensive steel instruments with which it is used. A really good article of Indian ink is somewhat difficult to find. Much of the ink in market is gritty, and instead of being a fine jet black, it is of a blueish-gray color. Moreover, notwithstanding all the grinding that the artist can give it, the particles are always coarse, and it does not readily sink into the paper. With such ink it is difficult to draw fine, clear, black lines, and utterly impossible to produce a soft mellow tint in shading. It is probable that the quality of the ink depends not only upon the materials from which it is made, but upon the method pursued in its manufacture, and in regard to both these points we are as yet wholly in the dark. When good Indian ink is wanted, therefore, the only method of securing it is to test carefully the various samples, until we get a good one, and then secure a supply that will last indefinitely. Fortunately the last is not a difficult thing to do, when we have found a sample that suits us; for a single stick of Indian ink, if carefully used, will last many years, even in the hands of a professional draughtsman. Of late years a liquid Indian ink has been introduced, and has given good satisfaction, but it is scarce and expensive. Since the ordinary Indian ink is made up with a fine animal glue, instead of mucilage made of vegetable gum, it very soon decomposes when ground up with water. Hence it can not be kept in bottles like ordinary ink, but must be prepared fresh whenever it is needed. As an ink for ordinary writing it is worthless, for the simple reason that it does not flow well, though for purposes where an absolutely indelible ink is needed—as, for instance, in writing out deeds and records—nothing better can be obtained. When used for this purpose, the addition of a *very* small quantity of caustic alkali—or, what is better yet, of ox-gall—causes it to flow freely and to sink deeply into the paper or other material used to receive it, provided the latter be not too heavily sized. When properly applied, neither heat, moisture, acids, alkalies, nor chemicals of any kind, affect it; and it might therefore be properly used to write those records which are placed under the corner-stones of important buildings, and which are expected to endure for an indefinite period.

The second class of inks comprises all those black inks and writing fluids that are commonly employed for commercial correspondence and records. The different formulæ for the preparation of ink that have been published, would fill a good sized volume; but most of the inks and writing fluids in market consist of a precipitate of gallate or tannate of iron, held in suspension by means of mucilage. Since iron may be used in either one of two distinct conditions when it is employed for the manufacture of ink, it follows that two distinct kinds of ink may be made from it. In one of these the iron is fully oxidated, and the ink is of a deep jet black. The precipitate of iron which exists in such ink seems to assume a coarse and heavy form, with a strong tendency to sink to the bottom of the containing vessel. It therefore requires a large proportion of mucilage to keep the coloring matter in suspension. The advantage which it possesses, is, that the ink is, from the very first, of a deep black; but on the other hand, the objections are quite as important, and consist in the fact that it can not be made to flow freely, and that it does not sink well into the paper, and is consequently easily removed. On the other hand, ink made with salts in which the iron exists as protoxide, is always pale at first, but afterwards assumes a dark hue; it flows freely and sinks well into the fibre, so that it is difficult to remove marks made by it. This character it is apt to lose, however, when exposed to the air, as we shall note when speaking of the preservation of ink.

In some cases a compromise is made, and the ink is prepared from materials, part of which only are in a state of complete oxidation. An attempt is thus made to secure an ink, which, while black from the first, will flow freely and sink well into the paper, and some very good inks are thus compounded.

Most of the inks known as violet, mauve, blue, red, carmine, etc., consist of true chemical solutions, generally nowadays of aniline, though the finest red ink is still made from carmine dissolved in ammonia. From the fact that there is no solid material to be kept in supension, these inks do not require mucilage in their composition provided they are used on paper that has a good deal of size in it; they consequently flow freely, do not leave a heavy streak of liquid behind the pen, and the streak that they do leave sinks almost instantly into the paper and disappears. In using them, no blotter is required; and they are, therefore, great favorites with authors and those persons who pay less regard to the color of their writing than to the ease with which the work is done, and the clearness and unblotted appearance which it presents. But from the fact that no really good black ink of this class has yet been produced, they have not come into general use amongst book-keepers and commercial men, and it must be acknowledged that on the whole a good black ink gives a better appearance to a set of books than ink of any other color.

Ink used for copying letters by means of the press, requires to be thicker than that used for ordinary writing, and therefore it is less pleasant to use; but the great advantage which attends the mechanical process of copying letters will always keep up the demand for it.

Such being the peculiar character of the inks in common use, it may be well to say a few words concerning the best methods of preserving them in good condition. The great enemies of all inks are evaporation, dust, and decomposition, and, in the case of iron inks, oxidation. The first difficulty can only be avoided by keeping the ink from exposure to the air, and this is best effected by adopting an inkstand in which the ink exposes a very small surface to the air. Many of the inkstands in use are made large at the base, for the purpose of rendering them difficult to overturn. In such stands the ink is spread out in a thin, wide layer, and not only evaporates rapidly, but where ordinary black ink is used, the iron oxidates, and the ink consequently deteriorates. A very common practice on the part of those who use ink, is to leave the mouth of the stand uncovered, in which case the ink becomes in a short time reduced to mud. All these difficulties may be in a measure avoided by using a heavy stand, having a small well or ink-holder, which should be kept well covered when not in use, and ought to be frequently cleaned, the old ink being thrown away. The supply of ink should be kept in a bottle, securely corked, and when the stand is filled, the new ink ought never to be poured into the old, as is generally done. Throw the old ink away; wash out the stand carefully, and fill it up with new fluid, and then you can enjoy the luxury of writing with ink that flows freely, and does not take half a minute to moisten the paper at each stroke that you attempt to make. To keep ink in good order, the stand should be washed out every two or three weeks.

Many inks, especially those made with iron and galls, are liable to mould and decompose. The formation of mould may, to a certain extent, be prevented by the use of creosote, carbolic acid, or cloves, and most of the better class of inks in market are prepared so as to resist this evil.

In the recipes generally given for making ink, it is recommended to *boil* the ingredients. A much better plan is to powder the galls and macerate them in cold water. By this latter process, more time is of course necessary to make it; but then the ink is very superior, and entirely free from extractive matter which has no inky quality, and which only tends to clog the pen and to turn the ink ropy and mouldy.

Black Ink.—1. In 1 gallon of water macerate 1 lb. of finely powdered Aleppo galls for two weeks, and strain off the liquid. Dissolve 5½ oz. sulphate of iron and 5 oz. gum arabic in as little water as is necessary, and mix the two liquids with constant stirring. Keep in a tall bottle, allow it to settle for some days, and it will be ready for use.

2. Take gall nuts, broken, one pound; sulphate of iron, half a pound; gum acacia and sugar candy, of each, a quarter of a pound; water, three quarts. Place the whole of these ingredients in a vessel where they can be agitated once a day; after standing for a fortnight or three weeks the ink is ready for use. Logwood and similar materials, are often advised to be used in conjunction with the gall nuts, but they serve no good purpose unless it be to make a cheaper article which fades rapidly.

3. It is said that the juice of elderberries to which sulphate of iron has been added, makes a good ink. The best formula is said to be 12½ pints juice and ½ oz. each sulphate of iron and crude pyroligneous acid.

Runge's Black Ink.—1. The original recipe of the inventor is as follows: Digest ¼ lb. logwood in chips for 12 hours in 3 pints boiling water. Simmer down gently to 1 quart, filter and add 20 grains yellow chromate of potassa.

2. The following modification of the above is more easily prepared: Dissolve 16 parts of extract of logwood in 1,000 parts of water, and add 1 part of neutral potassium chromate (yellow chromate of potassa).

Blue Ink.—Take 6 drachms pure Prussian blue and 1 drachm oxalic acid. Grind in a mortar with a little water until they form a perfectly smooth paste. Dissolve a sufficient quantity of this paste in water to give the proper tint.

Carmine Ink, French Process.—Take 22 grammes (4 grains) of the best carmine, add to it sixty-five grammes (2 ounces) of caustic ammonia, add one gramme (15½ grains) of white gum arabic. Leave the mixture until the gum is entirely dissolved. This ink is undoubtedly dearer than that prepared in the ordinary way, but it is incomparably more beautiful and more durable, for experience has proved that letters written with this ink, have for forty years been preserved without the slightest alteration.

Red Ink.—Boil ¼ lb. of Brazil wood, ¼ oz. of gum, ½ oz. of sugar, and ½ oz. of alum in a sufficient quantity of vinegar.

Aniline Inks.—The following formulæ for aniline inks are from recent authorities, and are said to give superior results:

Alcoholic Solutions.—1. General Formula: Dissolve 15 parts of aniline color in 150 parts of strong alcohol in a vessel of glass or enamelled iron for three hours; then add 1,000 parts distilled water; heat gently for some hours,—in fact, till the odor of the alcohol has quite disappeared; then add a solution consisting of 60 parts of powdered gum arabic in 250 parts of water.

2. Special Formula for Violet: Digest ½ oz. aniline violet in 1 oz. alcohol in a suitable vessel, as above, for three hours; then add 1 qt. of distilled water, and heat gently till odor of spirit is dissipated. Then add 2 drachms gum arabic dissolved in ½ pt. water, and allow the whole to settle. This will bear dilution, if desired, with an additional quantity of distilled water.

3. Special Formula for Blue: Dissolve 15 grains aniline blue in 1 oz. alcohol, and add 6 oz. in distilled water. Boil in proper vessel, as above, until odor of alcohol has disappeared. Then add 3 drachms powdered gum arabic dissolved in 4 oz. distilled water. Finally filter. It will be perceived that there is considerable difference in the above special formulæ, but there can be no harm in making it too strong, as it is no difficult matter to dilute with distilled water to taste.

Aqueous Solutions.—1. Magenta, 1 oz. to the gallon of boiling distilled water. 2. Violet: ½ oz. to a gallon ditto. 3. Blue: 1 oz. to 10 pts. ditto. 4. Green: 1 oz. to 5 pts. ditto.

The addition of a small quantity of vinegar will considerably improve the color of blue aniline fluid. These aqueous solutions are very enduring, though not exactly permanent, as they give way to long-continued exposure to sunlight. They are very limpid, dry quickly, and never clog. They should of course be filtered.

Gold Ink.—Grind gold-leaf with honey in a mortar until it is reduced to a fine powder. Wash out the honey with hot water and add mucilage of gum arabic. A cheap article may be made by using yellow bronze powder.

Silver Ink.—Prepared in the same way as gold ink, using silver leaf or silver bronze powder.

Marking Ink for Linen.—Dissolve ¼ oz. nitrate of silver in 1 oz. water and add strong liquid ammonia until the precipitate which is at first formed is redissolved. Add 1½ drachms gum mucilage and enough coloring matter to render the writing clearly visible. The writing is made black and indelible by passing a hot iron over it. Keep in the dark.

Indelible Aniline Ink.—Triturate 1½ grammes of aniline-black with 60 drops of strong hydrochloric acid and 42 or 43 grammes strongest alcohol; then add to it a hot solution of 2½ grammes gum arabic in 170 grammes of water.

This ink attacks steel pens but little. It is not destroyed either by strong mineral acids or by strong lye.

If the first alcoholic solution of aniline black be diluted with a solution of 2½ grammes of shellac in 140 grammes of alcohol (instead of gum arabic in 170 grammes of water) an ink is produced which may be employed for writing on wood, brass or leather, and which is remarkable for its deep black color.

Indelible Indian Ink.—Draughtsmen are well aware of the fact that lines drawn on paper with good India ink which has been well prepared, can not be washed out by mere sponging or washing with a brush. Now, however, it is proposed to take advantage of the fact that glue or gelatine, when mixed with bichromate of potassa, and exposed to the light, becomes insoluble, and thus renders India ink, which always contains a little gelatine, indelible. Reisenbichler, the discoverer, calls this kind of ink "Harttusch," or "hard India ink;" it is made by adding to the common article, when making, about one per cent., in a very fine powder, of bichromate of potash. This must be mixed with the ink in a dry state; otherwise, it is said, the ink could not be ground up easily in water. Those who can not provide themselves with ink prepared as above in the cake, can use a dilute solution of bichromate of potash in rubbing up the ink; it answers the same purpose, though the ink should be used thick, so that the yellow salt will not spread.

Indestructible Ink..—An ink that can not be erased with acids is obtained by the following recipe: To good gall ink add a strong solution of fine soluble Prussian blue in distilled water. This addition makes the ink, which was previously proof against alkalies, equally proof against acids, and forms a writing fluid which cannot be erased without destroying the paper. The ink writes greenish blue, but afterwards turns black.

Ink that will not Freeze.—It is said that a mixture of equal parts of concentrated glycerine, alcohol and water, deeply colored with aniline black, does not freeze in the coldest weather, flows freely from the pen, and does not spread. Our only fear would be that such ink would not dry thoroughly.

Sympathetic Ink or Secret Ink.—Write with thin solution of starch, and let the correspondent wash with solution of iodine.

2. Write with milk, onion juice or lemon juice, and let the correspondent expose to heat.

3. Write with solution of tartar emetic and wash with any alkaline sulphuret.

4. Brown.—On dissolving 1 part of potassium bromide, and 1 part of copper sulphate in 20 parts of water, and writing with the solution on paper, *very careful* heating will turn the writing brown.

5. Yellowish-green.—Writing done with a solution of 2 parts of potassium chromate, 2 of nitric acid, 2 of sodium chloride in 40 parts of water, turns yellowish-green on gentle warming.

6. Blue.—A solution of equal parts of sodium chloride and cobalt chloride in 20 times the amount of water produces lines which turn blue on gentle warming.

Letters may be written on postal cards with these inks, and will remain invisible until washed with the appropriate solution or exposed to heat. To prevent the letters from being seen by close scrutiny the solutions should be very dilute, and to distract the attention of those not in the secret, write some unimportant matter, in lines far apart, and between them write the private matter in secret or sympathetic ink.

Inks for Rubber Stamps and Stencils.—1. Black. Rub together one part of finest lampblack and 2 parts of Prussian blue with a little glycerin, then add 1 part powdered gum arabic, and enough glycerin to form a thin paste.

2. Carmine.—Dissolve 24 grains of carmine in 3 fl. oz. of water of ammonia, then add 2 fl. drachms of glycerin. Incorporate with this ½ oz. of powdered gum arabic.

3. Blue.—Rub together 6 parts of pure Prussian blue and 1 part oxalic acid with a little water, to a perfectly smooth paste. Let it stand in a rather warm place over night, then rub it with more water, and with 1 part of gum arabic to a thin paste.

4. Aniline inks may be made of any desired shade in the same manner. The best way of using these inks is by applying them, by means of a small pad, uniformly to a little cushion, on which the stamps are then inked.

The above formulæ have been tested by experience, and are said to give good results. Another set of formulæ, also highly recommended, is the following:

5. Black.—Finest lampblack, 10 parts; powdered gum arabic, 4 parts; glycerin, 4 parts; water, 3 parts. Dissolve the gum arabic in the water, add the glycerin, then rub the lampblack with the mixture in a mortar.

6. Colored.—Replace the lampblack in the above formula by the appropriate color; chrome-yellow for yellow; red lead or red ochre for red; green, ultramarine, or chrome-green for green; indigo or Prussian blue, or blue ultramarine for blue; umber for brown, etc.

Ink Eraser.

A good ink eraser is thus made: Take of chloride of lime, one pound, thoroughly pulverized, and four quarts of soft water. The above must be thoroughly shaken when first put together. It is required to stand twenty-four hours to dissolve the chloride of lime; then strain through a cotton cloth, after which add a teaspoonful of acetic acid to every ounce of the chloride of lime water. The eraser is used by reversing the penholder into the fluid, and applying it, without rubbing, to the word, figure, or blot required to be erased. When the ink has disappeared, absorb the fluid with a blotter, and the paper is immediately ready to write upon again. Chloride of lime has before been used with acids for the purpose as above proposed ; but in all previous processes the chloride of lime has been mixed with acids that burn and destroy the paper.

Inlaying.

Inlaying is a term applied to work in which certain figures which have been cut out of one kind of material are filled up with another of a different color. Such work is known as marquetry, and also as Boule work, and Reisner work, from the names of two famous French artists.

The simplest method of producing inlaid work in wood, is to take two thin boards, of wood or veneers, and glue them together with paper between, so that they may be easily separated again. Then, having drawn the required figures on them, cut along the lines with a very fine, hair-like saw. This process is known as *counterpart sawing*, and by it the pieces removed from one piece of wood, so exactly correspond with the perforations in the other piece, that when the two colors are separated and interchanged, the one material forms the ground and the other the inlay or pattern. If the saw be fine and the wood very dry when cut, but afterwards slightly damped when glued in its place, the joint is visible only on very close inspection, and then merely as a fine line. After being cut, the boards or veneers are separated (which is easily done by splitting the paper between them), and then glued in their places on the work which they are to ornament.

Imitation Inlaying.—Suppose an oak panel with a design inlaid with walnut is wanted. Grain the panel wholly in oil. This is not a bad ground for walnut. When the oak is dry, grain the whole of the panel in distemper. Have a paper with the design drawn thereon, the back of which has been rubbed with whiting, place it on the panel, and with a pointed stick trace the design. Then with a brush and quick varnish trace the whole of the design. When the varnish is dry, with a sponge and water remove the distemper, where the varnish has not touched. This, if well executed, presents a most beautiful imitation of inlaid wood. Marbles are executed in a similar manner.

Iron.

This is undoubtedly the most important metal used in the arts. Directions for working it, such at least as would be valuable to professional blacksmiths, would occupy more space than we can afford, and we therefore content ourselves with a few hints for amateurs.

Forging.—As a general rule, those who are not practical blacksmiths had better take their work to a smith's shop. Cases may, however, arise where it is necessary to forge some little job, and the following hints may prove of use.

In working iron a great deal depends upon the degree of heat to which it is raised. Blacksmiths distinguish five degrees, which they name as follows:

1. The black-red heat, just visible by daylight.
2. The low-red heat.
3. The bright red heat, when the black scales may be seen.
4. The white heat, when the scales are scarcely visible.
5. The welding heat, when the iron begins to burn with vivid sparks.

Of these temperatures the 1st, 2nd and 3rd are easily attained in a common stove or grate. It requires good management to secure the 4th in a common stove, and the 5th can hardly be obtained without a blast. The higher the temperature the softer and more easily worked the metal becomes, and the less liable to crack or split; and as good iron is not easily spoilt, like steel, by a high heat, it is always best to get the metal pretty soft.

Welding.—This operation requires considerable skill. The two great points to be attended to in making a perfect weld are that the metal shall be brought to a proper temperature, and that the surfaces to be united shall be perfectly clean. The latter point can only be secured by protecting the iron from the action of the air by means of some flux. Sand is generally used by blacksmiths and answers very well. When sand is brought into contact with oxide of iron at a high temperature, it combines with it and forms a fusible glass which flows over the surface of the iron and is easily driven out of the joint by pressure. Borax makes a still more fusible flux and may be successfully used by amateurs, but is too expensive for common use.

When two surfaces of iron, which have been cleansed by means of sand or borax, are brought together at a high heat and forcibly pressed into contact by hammering or pressure, they unite to form a solid mass. Bearing these principles in mind, a little practice will soon enable any one to make a respectable joint by welding.

Case-hardening.—This process is simply the conversion of the surface of a piece of iron into steel. Case-hardened articles, when plunged into cold water while highly heated, become as hard as the hardest steel, but they may be annealed and softened so as to be easily worked with files and turning tools, and afterwards hardened again so as to be as durable as ever. There are several processes for performing this operation. The following have been tested by experience:

1. Where it is desired that the articles should be hardened to a considerable depth: Char a quantity of bones, just enough (*and no more*) to enable you to powder them with a hammer. Lay a layer of this bone dust over the bottom of an iron tray or box, which may be easily made by bending heavy sheet iron into form. Lay the articles to be hardened on the bone dust, taking care that they do not touch each other. Cover with bone dust and fill up the tray with spent dust, charcoal or sand. Expose to a bright cherry red heat for half an hour or an hour, and then turn the entire contents of the tray into a vessel of cold water. We have seen beautiful results obtained by this process when carried out in a common kitchen stove.

Even raw bone dust, such as is sold for farming purposes, may be used with good results. Pieces of gas pipe make good receptacles to hold the work, the ends being stopped with iron plugs. When packing the articles in the tubes or trays, see that they do not touch each other.

Bone black or ivory black may also be used, and, as they may be purchased ready prepared, we may avoid the disagreeable process of roasting the raw material.

As this roasting of bones, leather, etc., gives rise to most abominable odors, the author of this manual some years ago devised the following preparation, which was found to give very excellent results. Prepare a strong solution of prussiate of potassa, boil in it as much coarsely-powdered wood charcoal as can be mixed with it. Drain off the superfluous liquid, spread the charcoal on a board, and dry by exposure to the air. When dry, roast it at a temperature just below that of ignition, the object being to drive off all moisture, but not to decompose the prussiate, which, at a red heat, is converted into cyanide of potassium and some other compounds. The charcoal thus prepared, and afterwards reduced to a moderately fine powder, will be found to answer quite as well as animal charcoal, and no difficulty will be found in case-hardening to a depth which will allow of a good deal of polishing before the soft metal underneath is reached.

2. Where mere superficial hardening is required, heat the article to be hardened to a bright red; sprinkle it liberally with powdered prussiate of potash. The salt will fuse, and if the piece of iron is small and gets cooled, heat it again and plunge into cold water.

Rust and Corrosion.—Iron is easily corroded by even the weak acids. Sulphuric acid, nitric acid, and hydrochloric acid all act on it quickly and powerfully. Air and moisture also quickly corrode it. It is a curious fact that carbonate of soda protects iron very perfectly from rust. We have seen a piece of iron that had been kept in a solution of soda for twenty years, and yet was quite bright.

There are several methods of protecting iron from rust. Painting, varnishing, tinning, zincing, etc., have all been tried with good effect. Painting and varnishing need no remarks. Where bright work is to be temporarily protected, however, a paint of white lead and tallow may be used. This will not dry, and may be easily and quickly removed with a little turpentine.

Zincing Iron.—The following is an excellent and cheap method for protecting from rust, iron articles exposed to the atmosphere, such as cramp-irons for stone, etc.: They are to be first cleansed by placing them in open wooden vessels, in water containing three-fourths to one per cent. of common sulphuric acid, and allowed to remain in it until the surface appears clean, or may be rendered so by scouring with a rag or wet sand. According to the amount of acid, this may require from six to twenty-four hours. Fresh acid must be added according to the extent of use and of the liquid; when this is saturated with sulphate of iron, it must be renewed. After removal from this bath, the articles are rinsed in fresh water, and scoured until they acquire a clean metallic surface, and then kept in water in which a little slaked lime has been stirred, until the next operation. When thus freed from rust, they are to be coated with a thin film of zinc, while cold, by means of chloride of zinc, which may be made by filling a glazed earthen vessel, of about two-thirds gallon capacity, three-fourths full of muriatic acid, and adding zinc clippings until effervescence ceases. The liquid is then to be turned off from the undissolved zinc, and preserved in a glass vessel. For use, it is poured into a sheet-zinc vessel, of suitable size and shape for the objects, and about 1·30 per cent. of its weight of finely powdered sal ammoniac added. The articles are then immersed in it, a scum of fine bubbles forming on the surface in from one to two minutes, indicative of the completion of the operation. The articles are next drained, so that the excess may flow back into the vessel. The iron articles thus coated with a fine film of zinc are placed on clean sheet iron, heated from beneath, and perfectly dried, and then dipped piece by piece, by means of tongs, into very hot (though not glowing) molten zinc, for a short time, until they acquire the temperature of the zinc. They are then removed and beaten, to cause the excess of zinc to fall off.

Cold Process for Zincing Iron.—The metal is first cleaned by being placed in a bath made up of water, 1,000 litres; chlorhydric acid, 550 litres; sulphuric acid, 50 litres; glycerine, 20 litres. On being removed from this bath, the metal is placed in a bath containing 10 per cent. of carbonate of potassa, and is next transferred to a metallizing bath, consisting of water, 1,000 litres; chloride of tin, 5 kilos.; chloride of zinc, 4 kilos.; bitartrate of potassa, 8 kilos.; acid sulphate of alumina, 4 kilos.; chloride of aluminum, 10 kilos. The metal is to be left in this mixture for from three to twelve hours, according to the thickness of the layer of zinc to be desired.

Tinning Iron.—The surface of the iron is cleaned from scale by vitriol or sulphuric acid, and then scoured with sand. It is now coated with a strong solution of chloride of zinc, and dipped into melted tin. The tin will instantly adhere to every spot that is clean.

Tinning Iron in the Cold.—The chief point which requires attention in this matter is that the tinning of iron in the cold cannot succeed at all, unless the bath contains, in solution or suspension, an organic substance like starch or glucose, although no precise scientific explanation of this indispensible condition has been hitherto given. To 100 litres of water are added 3 kilos. of rye meal; this mixture is boiled for half an hour, and next filtered through cloth; to the clear but thickish liquid are added 106 kilos. of pyrophosphate of soda, 17 kilos. of protochloride of tin in crystals (so-called tin-salt), 67 kilos. of neutral protochloride of tin, 100 to 120 grms. of sulphuric acid; this liquid is placed in well-made wooden troughs, and serves more especially for the tinning of iron and steel wire (previously polished) for the use of carding machines. When instead of the two sorts of tin just named, cyanide of silver and cyanide of potassium are taken, the iron is perfectly silvered.

Brightening Iron.—A Bavarian serial contains a method of brightening iron recommended by Boden. The articles to be brightened are, when taken from the forge or the rolls, in the case of such articles as plates, wire, etc., placed in dilute sulphuric acid (1 to 20), cleansing the articles, which are then washed clean with water and dried with sawdust. They are then dipped for a second or so in nitrous acid, washed carefully, dried in sawdust and rubbed clean. It is said that iron goods thus treated acquire a bright surface, having a white glance, without undergoing any of the usual polishing operations. This is a process that those interested can easily test for themselves. Boden states that the action of the sulphuric acid is increased by the addition of a little carbolic acid, but it is difficult to see what effect this can have, and it may very well be dispensed with.

To Remove the Blue Color Imparted to Iron and Steel by exposure to Heat.—Rub lightly with a sponge or rag dipped in diluted sulphuric, nitric, or hydrochloric acid. When the discoloration is removed, carefully wash the article, dry it by rubbing, warm it and give a coat of oil or it will rapidly rust.

Ivory.

Ivory is obtained from the tusk of the elephant, and although material nearly resembling it may be obtained from other animals, yet the true ivory stands unequalled as a material for ornamental turning and carving. It is not so brittle as bone, neither does it splinter so much when broken, and as it is entirely free from the vessels or pores which permeate all bone, the finished articles have a much more solid and even appearance. Although distinctly fibrous it cannot be torn up in filaments like bone or divided into thin leaves, except by the saw. It is in all respects the most suitable material for ornamental turning, as it is capable of receiving the most delicate lines and of being cut in the most slender proportions. But while it is thus valuable as a material for ornamental work, it is useless for any article requiring accuracy in its dimensions—such for example as the scales of draughtsmen and the graduated arcs of instruments for measuring angles. Owing to the great alterations which it sustains under slight atmospheric changes it cannot be relied upon, and has been condemned officially by the survey commissioners of almost all countries.

It is imagined by some that ivory may be softened so as to admit of being moulded like horn or tortoise shell. Its different analysis contradicts this expectation; thick pieces suffer no change in boiling water, thin pieces become a little more flexible, and thin shavings give off their jelly, which substance is occasionally prepared from them. It is true that the caustic alkali will act upon ivory as well as upon most animal substances, yet it only does so by decomposing it. Ivory, when exposed to the alkalies, first becomes unctuous or saponaceous on its outer surface, then soft, if in thin plates, and it may be ultimately dissolved provided the alkali be concentrated; but it does not in any such case resume its first condition.

Working and Polishing Ivory.—As a material to be worked by the mechanic, ivory stands midway between wood and brass, and is turned and cut by tools having more obtuse angles than those employed for wood, and yet sharper than those used for brass. It may be driven at a fair speed in the lathe, and is easily sawed by any saw having fine teeth.

The tools used for cutting and turning ivory should have their edges very finely finished on an oil stone so that they may cut smoothly and cleanly.

Turned works with plain surfaces may in general be left so smooth from the tool as to require but *very little polishing*, a point always aimed at with superior workmen by the employment of sharp tools. In the polishing of turned works very fine glass paper or emery paper is first used, and it is rendered still finer and smoother by rubbing two pieces together face to face; secondly, whiting and water as thick as cream is then applied on wash leather, linen, or cotton rag, which should be thin that the fingers may the more readily feel and avoid the keen fillets and edges of the ivory work, that would be rounded by excessive polishing; thirdly, the work is washed with clean water, applied by the same or another rag; fourthly, it is rubbed with a clean, dry cloth until all the moisture is absorbed, and, lastly, a very minute quantity of oil or tallow is put on the rag to give a gloss.

Scarcely any of the oil remains behind, and the apprehension of its being absorbed by the ivory and disposing it to turn yellow may be discarded; indeed the quantity of oil used is quite insignificant, and its main purpose is to keep the surface of the ivory slightly lubricated, so that the rag may not hang to it and wear it into rings or groovy marks. Putty powder is sometimes used for polishing ivory work, but it is more expensive and scarcely better suited than whiting, which is sufficiently hard for the purpose.

The polishing of irregular surfaces is generally done with a moderately hard nail brush, supplied with whiting and water, and lightly applied in all directions, to penetrate every interstice; after a period the work is brushed with plain water and a clean brush, to remove every vestige of the whiting. The ivory is dried by wiping and pressing it with a clean linen or cotton rag, and is afterwards allowed to dry in the air, or at a good distance from the fire; when dry a gloss is given with a clean brush on which a minute drop of oil is first applied.

It is better to do too little polishing at first, so as to need a repetition of the process, rather than by injudicious activity to round and obliterate all the delicate points and edges of the works, upon the preservation of which their beauty mainly depends.

Bleaching and Cleaning Ivory.—In reply to the question, What means there are of bleaching ivory which has become discolored? Holtzapffel, the great authority on such subjects, tells us that he regrets to be obliged to say that he is unacquainted with any of value. It is recommended in various popular works to scrub the ivory with Trent sand and water, and similar gritty materials; but these would only produce a sensible effect by the removal of the external surface of the material, which would be fatal to objects delicately carved by hand or with revolving cutting instruments applied to the lathe.

It is a well known fact that ivory suffers the least change

of color when it is exposed to the *light* and closely covered with a glass shade. It assumes its most nearly white condition when the oil with which it is naturally combined is recently evaporated; and it is the custom in some thin works, such as the keys of pianofortes, to hasten this period, by placing them for a few hours in an oven heated in a very moderate degree, although the more immediate object is to cause the pieces to shrink before they are glued upon the wooden bodies of the keys. Some persons boil the transparent ivory in pearl-ash and water to whiten it; this appears to act by the superficial extraction of the oily matter as in bone, although it is very much better not to resort to the practice, which is principally employed to render that ivory which is partly opaque and partly transparent, of more nearly uniform appearance. It is more than probable, however, that the discoloration of ivory is due to the oil which it contains or has absorbed, and which becomes yellow and rancid, and every effort should be made to prevent oily or greasy bodies from coming in contact with ivory. Thus the keys of a pianoforte should be kept clean by carefully washing from the fingers the natural grease which all skin gives out. When ivory keys become very yellow they may be considerably whitened by allowing a paste of whiting, slightly moistened with potash, to lie on them for twenty-four hours. The potash extracts the oil which is absorbed by the chalk and may be thus removed.

It is a well known fact that most oils and resins may be bleached by exposure to sunlight. It is by this means that opticians render Canada balsam clear and transparent. It has been found that pieces of apparatus made of ivory, such as rules, etc., which have become yellow by age, may be bleached by dipping them in turpentine and exposing them to sunlight.

The fumes of sulphur, chloride of lime, etc., though frequently recommended, are of no value as bleachers of ivory.

Javelle Water.

This name was derived from the town of *Javelle*, in France, where a manufactory sold a liquor which had the property of bleaching cloth by an immersion of some hours only. The following is the original recipe given by Gray in his "Operative Chemist": $2\frac{1}{4}$ lbs. common salt, 2 lbs of sulphuric acid, and ¾ lb. of black manganese are mixed in a retort and heated, and the gas which comes over is condensed in 2 gallons of water in which 5 lbs. of potash have been dissolved. This liquor is diluted with twelve times its bulk of water.

This process is available only by chemists, however. The following gives good results : Take 4 lbs. carbonate of soda, and 1 lb. chloride of lime ; put the soda into a kettle, add 1 gallon of boiling water and boil for from 10 to 15 minutes ; then stir in the chloride of lime, breaking down all lumps with a wooden spatula or stirrer. Pour into large glass bottles ; when cold and settled it will be ready for use.

This forms a very efficient bleaching liquid and one which it is not difficult to remove from the bleached fabric. Old and stained engravings and books, as well as linen and cotton goods that have become yellow with dirt and age, may be rendered snowy white by the application of this liquid

Jewelry and Gilded Ware.

Ordinary gold jewelry may be effectually cleansed by washing with soap and warm water, rinsing in cold water and drying in warm boxwood sawdust. Plain, smooth surfaces may be rubbed with chamois leather charged either with rouge or prepared chalk, but the less rubbing the better.

Silver is liable to tarnish by the action of sulphur, and where there is fine chased or engraved work the extreme delicacy of the lines may be injured by much rubbing. In such cases the articles may be cleaned by washing with a solution of hyposulphite of soda. Cyanide of potassium is a more powerful cleansing agent but is very poisonous.

In cleaning gilded ware, different processes must be used for articles gilded by fire or by the galvanic process, and articles gilded by gold leaf, such as frames, etc. For cleaning articles gilded by the first-named methods, one part of borax is dissolved in sixteen parts of water. With this solution the article is carefully rubbed by means of a soft sponge or brush, then rinsed with water, and finally dried with a linen rag, or if small, such as a piece of jewelry, with boxwood sawdust. If at all convenient, the article is warmed previously to being rubbed, by which means the brilliancy of it is greatly increased. In cleaning gilded frames of the last named order, pure water only must be employed, and the rubbing off of the impurities must take place by means of a very slight pressure. Wares of imitation gilt are generally covered with a shellac or resin varnish, which would be dissolved by the application of soap water, alkaline solutions, or spirits of wine. Were the varnish rubbed off, the exceedingly thin layer of gold or silver leaf beneath would also disappear. In our experience we have seen hundreds of once valuable but now worthless frames, they having become thus simply by the application of soap water.

Lacquer.

Lacquer is so called because it usually contains gum *lac*, either shellac or seed lac. Seed lac is the original form of the gum or resin; after being purified it is moulded into thin sheets, like shell, and hence is called *shellac*. Shellac is frequently bleached so as to become quite white, in which state it forms a colorless solution. Bleached shellac is never as strong as the gum in its natural condition, and unless it be fresh it neither dissolves well in alcohol nor does it preserve any metal to which it may be applied.

There are many recipes for good lacquer, but the success of the operator depends quite as much upon skill as upon the particular recipe employed. The metal must be cleaned perfectly from grease and dirt, and in lacquering new work it is always best to lacquer as soon after polishing as possible. Old lacquer may be removed with a strong lye of potash or soda, after which the work should be well washed in water, dried in fine beech or boxwood sawdust and polished with whiting, applied with a soft brush. The condition of the work, as to cleanliness and polish, is perhaps the most important point in lacquering.

The metal should be heated and the lacquer applied evenly with a soft camel hair brush. A temperature of about that of boiling water will be found right.

The solution of lac or varnish is colored to suit the requirements or taste of the user.

A good pale lacquer consists of three parts of Cape aloes and one of turmeric to one of simple lac varnish. A full yellow contains four of turmeric and one of annatto to one of lac varnish. A gold lacquer, four of dragon's-blood and one of turmeric to one of lac varnish. A red, thirty-two parts of annatto and eight of dragon's-blood to one of lac varnish.

A great deal depends, also, upon the depth of color imparted to the lacquer, and as this may require to be varied, a very good plan is to make up a small stock bottle, holding, say, half a pint, according to any good recipe, and add as much of it to the varnish as may be required for the desired tint.

The following are a few favorite recipes:

Deep Gold Lacquer.—Alcohol, ½ pint; dragon's-blood, 1 drachm; seed lac, 1½ oz.; turmeric, ¼ oz. Shake up well for a week, at intervals of, say, a couple of hours; then allow to settle, and decant the clear lacquer; and if at all dirty filter through a tuft of cotton wool. This lacquer may be diluted with a simple solution of shellac in alcohol and will then give a paler tint.

Bright Gold Lacquer.—1. Turmeric, 1 oz.; saffron ¼ oz.; Spanish annatto, ¼ oz.; alcohol, 1 pint. Digest at a gentle heat for several days; strain through coarse linen; put the tincture in a bottle and add 3 oz. good seed lac coarsely powdered. Let it stand for several days, shaking occasionally. Allow to settle and use the clear liquid.

2. Take 1 oz. annatto and 8 oz. alcohol. Mix in a bottle by themselves. Also mix separately 1 oz. gamboge and 8 oz. alcohol. With these mixtures color seed lac varnish to suit yourself. If it be too red add gamboge; if too yellow add annatto; if the color be too deep, add spirit. In this manner you may color brass of any desired tint.

Pale Gold Lacquer.—Best pale shellac (picked pieces), 8 oz.; sandarac, 2 oz.; turmeric, 8 oz.; annatto, 2 oz.; dragon's-blood, ¼ oz.; alcohol, 1 gallon. Mix, shake frequently till the gums are dissolved and the color extracted from the coloring matters and then allow to settle.

Lacquer used by A. Ross.—4 oz. shellac and ¼ oz. gamboge are dissolved by agitation, without heat, in 24 oz. pure pyro-acetic ether. The solution is allowed to stand until the gummy matters, not taken up by the spirit, subside. The clear liquor is then decanted, and when required for use is mixed with 8 times its quantity of alcohol. In this case the pyro-acetic ether is employed for dissolving the shellac in order to prevent any but the purely resinous portions being taken up, which is almost certain to occur with ordinary alcohol; but if the lacquer were made entirely with pyro-acetic ether, the latter would evaporate too rapidly to allow time for the lacquer to be equally applied.

Lacquers suffer a chemical change by heat and light, and must, therefore, be kept in a cool place and in dark vessels. The pans used should be either of glass or earthenware, and the brushes of camel's hair with no metal fittings.

Laundry Gloss.

Various recipes have been given for imparting a fine gloss to linen. Gum arabic, white wax, spermaceti, etc., have all been highly recommended, and are, no doubt, useful to a certain extent, but the great secret seems to lie in the quality of the iron used and the skill of the laundress. If the iron is hard, close grained and finely polished, the work will be much easier. Laundresses always have a favorite smoothing iron with which they do most of their work, and many of them have the front edge of the iron rounded so that great pressure can be brought to bear on a very small spot instead of being spread over a space the size of the whole face of the iron. If smoothing irons have become rough and rusty it will pay to send them to a grinder to have them not only ground but *buffed* (see aritcle on *Polishing Metals*). The greatest care should be taken not to allow them to get spotted with rust, and they should never be "brightened" with coarse sand, ashes, emery, etc. If it is necessary to polish them, rub them on a board, or preferably a piece of leather charged with the finest flour of emery, obtained by washing, or better still, jeweller's rouge.

Leaves—Skeleton.

The following is a simple method of preparing skeleton leaves, and is decidedly preferable to the old and tedious method of maceration, as it is quite as efficient and not at all offensive. First dissolve four ounces of common washing soda in a quart of boiling water, then add two ounces of slaked quicklime and boil for about fifteen minutes. Allow the solution to cool: afterwards pour off all the clear liquor into a clean saucepan. When this liquor is at its boiling heat place the leaves carefully in the pan, and boil the whole together for an hour, adding from time to time enough water to make up for the loss by evaporation. The epidermis and parenchyma of some leaves will more readily separate than others. A good test is to try the leaves after they have been gently boiling for an hour, and if the cellular matter does not easily rub off betwixt the finger and thumb beneath cold water, boil them again for a short time. When the fleshy matter is found to be sufficiently softened, rub them separately but very gently beneath cold water until the perfect skeleton is exposed.

The skeletons, at first, are of a dirty white color; to make them of a pure white, and therefore more beautiful, all that is necessary is to bleach them in a weak solution of chloride of lime—a large teaspoonful of chloride of lime to a quart of water; if a few drops of vinegar are added to the solution it is all the better, for then the free chlorine is liberated. Do not allow them to remain too long in the bleaching liquor, or they will become too brittle, and cannot afterwards be handled without injury. About fifteen minutes will be sufficient to make them white and clean looking. Dry the specimens in white blotting paper, beneath a gentle pressure. Simple leaves are the best for young beginners to experiment on; the vine, poplar, beach and ivy leaves make excellent skeletons. Care must be exercised in the selection of leaves, as well as the period of the year and the state of the atmosphere when the specimens are collected; otherwise, failure will be the result. The best months to gather the specimens are July and August. Never collect specimens in damp weather, and none but perfectly matured leaves ought to be selected.

Lights—Signal and Colored.

The following recipes are from the United States Ordnance Manual, and may be considered reliable. The composition for signal lights is packed in shallow vessels of large diameter so as to expose considerable surface. Where the burning surface is large, the light attains great intensity, but the material burns out rapidly. In arranging the size and shape of the case, therefore, regard must be had to the time the light is expected to burn and the brilliancy that is wanted. [*See caution at end of this article.*]

Bengal Light.—Antimony, 2; sulphur, 4; mealed powder, 4; nitrate of soda, 16.

Blue.—Black sulphuret of antimony, 1; sulphur, 2; pure nitre, 6. Grind to a very fine powder and mix thoroughly. See that the nitre is perfectly dry. This composition gives a bluish white light; a deeper blue may be had by the addition of a little finely pulverized zinc.

Red.—1. Saltpetre, 5 ; sulphur, 6 ; nitrate of strontia, 20 ; lampblack, 1.

2. Nitrate of strontia, 20 ; chlorate of potassa, 8 ; Sulphur, 6 ; charcoal, 1.

White.—Saltpetre, 16 ; sulphur, 8 ; mealed powder, 4. Grind to a very fine powder and mix well.

The following have been very highly recommended :

Crimson Fire.—Sulphide of antimony, 4 ; chlorate of potassa, 5 ; powdered roll brimstone, 13 ; dry nitrate of strontia, 40 parts.

A very little charcoal added to the above makes it burn quicker.

Green Fire.—Fine charcoal, 3 ; sulphur, 13 ; chlorate of potassa, 8 ; nitrate of baryta, 77.

White.—1. Nitrate of potassa (saltpetre), 24 ; sulphur 7 ; charcoal, 1.

2. Nitre, 6 ; sulphur, 2 ; yellow sulphuret of arsenic, 1. [NOTE.—This light is a very brilliant one and a very pure white, but the fumes are highly poisonous. It should be used only in the open air and the wind should blow the vapors away from the spectators—not towards them.]

3. Chlorate of potash, 10 ; nitre, 5 ; lycopodium, 3 ; charcoal 2.

4. Metallic magnesium in the form of ribbon or wire. This is the best and most easily used. It may be purchased of most dealers in chemicals. A few inches of magnesium ribbon coiled into a spiral (like a spiral spring) and ignited by means of a spirit lamp, or even by a little tuft of cotton soaked in alcohol and fired with a lucifer match, makes a light of surpassing brilliancy and power. It requires a slight knack to ignite the ribbon. Hold the end of it steadily in the *outer edge* of the flame and it will soon take fire. The light given out by a small ribbon of magnesium is clearly visible at a distance of thirty miles.

Lights for Indoor Illuminations.—Many of the above are unfit for indoor exhibitions owing to the amount of sulphurous gas given off. For tableaux in churches, schools and private houses, the best light is undoubtedly magnesium or, where it can be had, the lime light (sometimes, though erroneously, called the calcium light). Both of these lights are very powerful, and any color may be obtained by the use of pieces of differently colored glass. A very effective arrangement consists of a tin box, which may be made out of one of those cases in which crackers are imported. Procure good-sized pieces of red and blue glass, the red being a soft, warm tint, such as will add a richness to the complexions of those upon whom the light is thrown. Arrange one end of the tin box so that these glasses may be slipped over a large hole in it. The opposite end of the box should be highly polished so as to act as a reflector, and a hole should be cut in one side so as to allow of the introduction of the magnesium.

In every case the burning matter should be so shaded that it may not be seen by the audience. If the direct light from the burning body meets the eyes of the spectators the reflected light from the objects composing the tableau will have no effect.

Where arrangements for lime or magnesium lights cannot be made, the following may be used.

White.—Chlorate of potash, 12; nitre, 5; finely powdered loaf sugar, 4; lycopodium 2.

Green.—Nitrate of baryta, shellac and chlorate of potassa, all finely powdered, equal parts by bulk.

Red.—Nitrate of strontia, shellac and chlorate of potassa, all finely powdered, equal parts by bulk.

The brilliancy of these fires will depend largely upon the thoroughness with which the materials are finely powdered and mixed. [*See caution at end of this article.*]

Braunschweizer recommends the following formulæ as giving excellent results, the lights being good without producing injurious fumes:

Red.—Nitrate of strontia, 9; shellac, 3; chlorate of potassa, 1½.

Green.—Nitrate of baryta, 9; shellac, 3; chlorate of potassa, 1½.

Blue.—Ammoniacal sulphate of copper, 8; chlorate of potassa, 6; shellac, 1.

The *Pharmacist* gives the following formula for "Red Fire," which will not evolve sulphurous acid during combustion: nitrate of strontia, 1 lb.; chlorate of potassa, ¼ lb.; shellac, ¼ lb.

These ingredients must be thoroughly dried, powdered separately, and carefully mixed by gentle stirring.

Ghosts, Demons, Spectres and Murderers.—To give a ghastly

hue to the faces of the actors, the best light is that produced by some salt of soda, common salt being very good. We have succeeded well in this way : A piece of wire gauze such as ash-sifters are made of, and about a foot square, was supported at a height of about a foot from the floor, which was protected by a sheet of iron. On the wire gauze were laid twenty-five wads of cotton waste which had been soaked in a solution of common salt, dried and dipped in alcohol just before being laid on the wire. When these were ignited we had twenty-five powerful flames all tinged with sodium and burning freely, as the air rose readily among them through the wire grating. Such a flame produces quite a powerful light and gives a death-like appearance to even the most rosy-cheeked girl.

The following give a strong light and produce a most ghastly effect:

1. Nitrate of soda, 10 ; chlorate of potash, 10 ; sulphide of antimony, 3 ; shellac, 4. The materials must be warm and dry, and as the nitrate of soda attracts moisture rapidly, it must be well dried, then finely powdered as quickly as possible and kept in well-corked bottles. As this gives off a good deal of sulphurous fumes, the following may be preferred where the ventilation is not good :

2. Nitrate of soda, 10 ; chlorate of potassa, 15 ; white sugar finely powdered, 5 ; lycopodium, 2.

CAUTION.

In using chlorate of potassa the greatest care is necessary. It may be powdered and otherwise handled safely when alone, but when combustible matter of any kind is added to it, the mixture becomes highly explosive and must be very gently handled. It must therefore be powdered *separately* and only mixed with the other ingredients *after* they have been powdered. The mixing should be done on a large sheet of paper, very gently, but very thoroughly, with a thin, broad-bladed knife.

Mixtures of chlorate of potash with sulphur, sulphurets, and especially phosphorous, are liable to explode spontaneously after a time, and should never be kept on hand. They should be made as wanted.

Flowers of sulphur are very liable to contain a trace of sulphuric or sulphurous acid, which, acting upon chlorate of potash causes spontaneous ignition. This may be obviated by pouring a few drops of liquid ammonia on the sulphur, mixing it up thoroughly and allowing it to stand for some time. A safe way also is to use powdered roll brimstone instead of flowers of sulphur.

Phosphorous Light.—One of the most brilliant lights known is produced by burning phosphorous in oxygen. The apparatus usually employed for this purpose is bulky and expensive, but the following is a very simple method of producing a very intense light by the combustion of phosphorous: Take an amount of nitre proportional to the desired intensity and duration of the light required, dry it thoroughly, powder it and pack it solidly in an earthen vessel, leaving a small cup-like hollow in its upper surface. In this hollow place a piece of phosphorous which has been carefully dried with soft paper or rags and set it on fire. As the phosphorous burns, the nitre melts, decomposes and furnishes it with pure oxygen, and the resulting light is very brilliant.

NOTE.—In handling phosphorous be very careful. Do not touch it with the hands or *rub* it with the article used to dry it, as it takes fire very easily, and the burns produced by it are very severe. It should always be cut under water.

Photographic Light.—A light of intense photographic power is produced by burning bisulphide of carbon in an argand lamp and passing a stream of nitric oxide through the centre of the flame. Nitric oxide is easily produced as wanted by allowing nitric acid to act on scraps of copper.

The following specific directions will enable the reader to produce this light in a less simple but more effective manner: A quart bottle with a somewhat large mouth, has a cork with two openings. Through one of these a tube passes to near the bottom of the bottle; through the second a large tube packed with iron scale issues. Fragments of pumice fill the bottle, and on these carbon disulphide is poured. A current of nitric oxide gas, prepared by Deville's method—by the action of nitric and sulphuric acids on metallic iron contained in a self-regulating reservoir—is passed through the bottle, where it takes up the vapor of the disulphide. It is then led through the safety-tube, packed with iron-scale, to a gas burner of the required capacity. Excellent photographs have been taken in five seconds with this light, the object being six feet distant. In photographic power the light is asserted to be superior to the magnesium or calcium light, and even to surpass the electric light itself. The products of combustion are noxious and must be gotten rid of.

Chatham Light.—This is a most intense flash-light used for military signals. Three parts finely powdered resin are mixed with one part magnesium dust, and blown by means of a tube through the flame of a spirit lamp. The flame should be large so as to insure the ignition of all the dust. The distance at which such a flame can be seen is extraordinary.

Some years ago the author devised a method of producing a light of marvellous brilliancy by the use of magnesium powder. A rude argand spirit lamp was constructed in such a way that the central tube could be connected in an air-tight fashion with a reservoir of oxygen. A small stopcock, with the hole of the plug closed at one side so as to leave a *cup* instead of a hole, was fitted into the tube leading from the oxygen reservoir to the lamp. When turned upward this cup was easily filled with magnesium powder, and when turned down it of course dropped its charge into the stream of oxygen, which carried it at once to the lamp, there to be consumed in a flash of extraordinary brilliancy.

Looking Glass. (*See Mirrors.*)

Lubricators.

In selecting a lubricator for any rubbing surfaces, care must be taken to adapt the character of the lubricating material to the nature of the rubbing surfaces and the weight which they have to sustain. A fine, thin oil is useless for heavy bearings, and a hard, stiff soap, which would be excellent for such bearings, would be a poor article for a very light piece of machinery. In the case of heavy bearings, such as railway axles, when they once begin to heat and cut, it will be found impossible to prevent heating by the mere application of oil. The surfaces of the metal must be worked over either by grinding or the turning tool. Thus, when journals heat at sea, the usual custom is to use sulphur, black-lead, or water; but the relief they afford is only temporary. The following is a method that gives permanent relief: When you find the journals getting hot, slack back the nuts on the cap from one-quarter to one-third of a turn, and supply the journal freely with dust procured by rubbing two Bath bricks together, mixed in oil to a consistency a little thinner than cream. After a short time begin cautiously to set up on the nuts; and before finally bringing the nuts to their original position, give a copious supply of oil alone to wash out the journal; then bring the nuts into position, and you will have no further trouble. This plan has also been tried on railway journals, and it has been found that a handful of clay or gravel has effected that which gallons of oil and water could not do.

In addition to the usual oils and grease the following lubricators deserve attention:

1. *Plumbago.*—This material is gradually coming into use, and when properly selected and applied it never fails to give satisfactory results. It may be used on the heaviest planers and ocean steamers, or on the lightest watchwork. When applied to delicate machinery the surfaces should be very lightly coated with the plumbago by means of a brush. In this way all danger of grit is avoided. Plumbago seems to be specially adapted to diminish the friction between porous surfaces, such as wood and cast iron. For the cast iron beds of heavy planers it is a specific.

2. *Anti-Attrition.*—Mix 4 lbs. tallow or soap with 1 lb. finely ground plumbago. The best lubricator for wood working on wood. Excellent for wooden screws where great power is required.

3. *Fine Lubricating Oil.*—Put fine olive oil in a bottle with scrapings of lead and expose it to the sun for a few weeks. Pour off the clear oil for use. Another method is to freeze fine olive oil, strain out the liquid portion and preserve for use.

Booth's Axle Grease.—Dissolve ½ lb. washing soda in 1 gallon water and add 3 lbs. tallow and 6 lbs. palm oil. Heat to 210° Fahr., and keep constantly stirring until cooled to 60° or 70°.

Marble.

Marble is a compact carbonate of lime which varies in color, some specimens being pure white, others perfectly black, while others are green, red, veined, mottled, etc. The famous Mexican onyx, so-called, is also a carbonate of lime, and notwithstanding its hardness and beauty is liable to injury from the same causes that affect ordinary marble.

Marble is easily dissolved, with escape of carbonic acid gas, by the mineral acids, sulphuric, nitric, hydrochloric, etc., and it is also acted upon, though more slowly by vinegar, the acids of fruit, etc. It is also soluble in water containing an excess of carbonic acid, and therefore dissolves rapidly in the ordinary "soda" water that is so generally sold as a beverage, for this fluid, in its pure state, consists solely of water holding a large amount of carbonic acid in solution. Consequently bottles and glasses of this liquid should not be placed where there is any danger of spilling it on mantel pieces, table tops, etc., as it will infallibly destroy the exquisite polish upon which the beauty of such articles of furniture depends.

Finely carved articles of marble, when exposed to the rain of our northern climates, are apt to suffer corrosion, and the delicate tracery of the sculptor is soon lost. Therefore, while marble answered very well in the comparatively dry climates of Greece and Egypt, it is unsuited for statues, etc., exposed to the open air, in England and America, the rainfall in these countries being very great, and the moisture heavily charged with carbonic and sulphurous acids.

In cleaning marble ornaments, etc., great care must be exercised to use nothing corrosive like acids, chlorides, or metallic salts, such as are usually recommended for removing stains of inks and dyes from wood and textile fabrics. When marble has been stained by ink or vegetable coloring matter, the only way to remove it is to apply warm water abundantly and for a long time. If the marble is very compact, and the stain consequently quite superficial, the article may be scraped and repolished, but of course this is applicable only to objects which have plane surfaces, or those with simple curves. Elaborately carved or sculptured objects could not be so treated.

Greasy stains may be removed by covering them with a paste of chalk and potash or soda. The alkali will convert the grease into soap, which will be gradually absorbed by the chalk and thus removed. In such cases, however, the stains, especially if old, may require a long time and several repetitions of the process. Alkalies (potash, soda and ammonia) may be applied to marble without injuring it, and any stains which they can remove may be taken out by their means.

Marble is easily worked either on the bench or in the lathe

In the latter case, however, great care must be taken to avoid anything like a heavy cut, since marble is so rigid and brittle that if the cut be heavy the article is apt to be broken. The only tool that can be used is a steel point, tempered to a straw color. The tool requires frequent grinding, and when it gets broad it must be forged over again, as a flat tool will not turn marble at all.

For working and finishing marble on the bench the following is the process: After the marble is sawn into slab, the first operation is to grind it down with a flat coarse sandstone and water, or with an iron plate, fed with fine sand and water, until all the marks of the saw are perfectly removed; secondly, a fine sandstone is used with water until the marks made by the first stone are removed; thirdly, a finer sandstone is applied to work out the marks of the former; fourthly, pumice stone with water, and fifthly, snake stone is used, and this last finishes what is called the *grounding*.

Next comes the polishing, which is principally performed with rollers of woolen cloth or list made to the size of about three inches diameter. As the sixth process, a rubber is charged with flour emery and a moderate degree of moisture; this rubber is worked uniformly over every part until the marble acquires a kind of greasy polish; seventhly, the work is completed with a similar roll of cloth charged with putty powder and water. Some prefer, as the polisher, an old cotton stocking not made into a rubber, and in some few of the more delicate works crocus is used intermediately between the emery and the putty powder. It is necessary to wash the marble after each operation, so that not a particle of the previous polishing material may remain, otherwise the work will be scratched.

The dull parts of sculpture are finished in four different manners, or rather the complete process of smoothing is discontinued at various stages so as to form four gradations, which may be described as follows:

First.—The marble is sometimes left from the long and very slender statuary's chisel, the reverse end of which is formed with a sharp circular edge or ridge, just like a hollow centre, in order that the metal hammer, which is of soft iron, tin or zinc, may be slightly indented by the chisel, so as to avoid its glancing off; the chisel marks leave the surface somewhat rough and matted, intermediate between the granular and crystalline character.

Secondly.—For surfaces somewhat smoother, rasps are used to remove the ridges left by the chisel; the rasps leave a striated or lined effect suitable for draperies, and which is made more or less regular according to the uniformity of the strokes, or the reverse.

Thirdly.—Files are employed for still smoother surfaces of the same character; and it is to be observed that the files and rasps are generally curved at the ends, to adapt them to the curvilinear forms of the sculpture.

Fourthly.—For the smoothest of the dull or unpolished surfaces, the faint marks left by the file are rubbed out with Trent sand or silver sand and water, applied by means of a stick of deal cut to a point, and rubbed all over the work in little irregular circles, as a child would scribble on a slate, and if the end of the stick is covered with two or three thicknesses of cloth the marble receives a still rounder or softer effect than from the naked stick, for which the cabbage wood or partridge wood is sometimes used, and the end of the stick is slightly bruised, so that the fibres of the wood may assume the character of the stiff brush, known by artists as a scrub.

Mr. Thomas Smith tells us that he has successfully copied the minute roughness or granulation of the skin, by a kind of etching which he was induced to try, by imagining that he could trace such a process to have been used in some of the most perfect of the ancient marbles that had not been exposed to the open air. The work having been smoothed with sand, as above, he takes a hard, stubby brush and therewith dots the marble with muriatic acid, and which quickly, yet partially, dissolves the surface. The strength of the acid, which must not be excessive, is tested upon a piece of waste marble; the brush is hastily dipped in the acid, applied to the work, quickly rinsed in water, and then used for removing the acid from the marble. It is obvious the process calls for a certain admixture of dexterity and boldness, and sometimes requires several repetitions, the process occupying only a few minutes each time.

Fifthly.—The bright parts of sculpture. Few of the works in sculpture are polished, and such as are, are required in the first instance to pass through the four stages already explained for producing the smooth but dull surface; after which, slender square pieces of the second gritstone and of snakestone are used with water as a pencil, and then fine emery and putty powder on sticks of wood; but the work is exceedingly tedious, and requires very great care, that the artistical character of the work, and any keen edges that may be required are not lost in the polishing.

Metals—Polishing.

Metals are polished either by burnishing or buffing. The process of burnishing consists in rubbing down all the minute roughnesses by means of a highly polished steel or agate tool—none of the metal being removed.

The action of the burnisher appears to depend upon two circumstances; first, that the harder the material to be polished the greater lustre it will receive; the burnisher is, therefore, commonly made of *hardened steel*, which exceeds in hardness nearly every metallic body. And secondly, its action depends on the intimacy of the contact betwixt the burnisher and the work; and the pressure of the brightened burnisher being, in reality, from its rounded or elliptical section, exerted upon only one mathematical line or point of the work at a time, it acts with great pressure and in a manner distinctly analogous to the steel die used in making coin; in which latter case the dull but smooth blank becomes instantly the bright and lustrous coin, in virtue of the intimate contact produced in the coining press between the entire surface of the blank and that of the highly polished die.

It by no means follows, however, that the burnisher will produce highly finished surfaces, unless they have been previously rendered smooth, and proper for the application of this instrument, as a rough surface, having any file marks or scratches, will exhibit the original defects, notwithstanding that they may be glossed over with the burnisher which follows every irregularity; and excessive pressure, which might be expected to correct the evil as in coining, only fills the work with furrows, or produces an irregular indented surface, which by workmen is said to be *full of utters*.

Therefore, the greater the degree of excellence that is required in burnished works, the more carefully should they be smoothed before the application of the burnisher, and this tool should also be cleaned on a buff stick with crocus immediately before use; and it should in general be applied with the least degree of friction that will suffice. Cutlers mostly consider that burnishers for steel are best rubbed on a buff stick with the finest flour emery; for silver, however, they polish the burnisher with crocus as usual. Most of the metals, previously to their being burnished, are rubbed with oil to lessen the risk of tearing or scratching them, but for gold and silver the burnisher is commonly used dry, unless soap and water or skimmed milk are employed; and for brass furniture, beer or water, with or without a little vinegar, is preferred for lubricating the burnisher.

Buffing is performed by rubbing the metal with soft leather, which has been charged with very fine polishing powder. The rubbing is sometimes done by hand, but more frequently the buff is made into a wheel which revolves rapidly in a lathe and the work is held against it.

The polishing powder that is selected must be chosen with special reference to the metal that is to be buffed. Thus, for steel and brass the best polishing powder is crocus or rouge, which may be purchased of any dealer in tools, or may be made by exposing very clean and pure crystals of sulphate of iron to heat, according to the directions given hereafter under the head of *Polishing Powders*. The hardest part of the rouge must be selected, and great care must be taken to have it clean and free from particles of dust and sand, which would inevitably scratch the article to be polished and render it necessary to again repeat all the previous processes of filing, grinding, etc.

Soft metals like gold and silver may be polished with comparatively soft powders, such as prepared chalk or putty powder (oxide of tin).

When metals are to be polished in the lathe the process is very simple. After being turned or filed smooth the article is still further polished by means of fine emery and oil, applied with a stick, and in the case of rods or cylinders, a sort of clamp is used so that great pressure can be brought to bear on the part to be polished. The work must be examined from time to time to see that all parts are brought up equally to the greatest smoothness and freedom from scratches, and as fast as this occurs polishing powder of finer and finer quality is used, until the required finish is attained.

In polishing metals or any other hard substances by

abrasion, the great point is to bring the whole surface up equally. A single scratch will destroy the appearance of the finest work, and it cannot be removed except by going back to the stage to which it corresponds, and beginning again from that point. Thus, if in working with a smooth file we make a scratch as deep as the cut of a bastard file, it is of no use to try and remove this scratch with the smooth file, we must go back, and taking a bastard file make the surface as even as possible with it, and afterwards work forward through fine files and polishing powders.

Mirrors.

As it is frequently convenient to be able to silver a piece of glass for a special purpose, we quote from Faraday's work on Chemical Manipulation, the following directions for performing this operation:

A piece of clean, smooth tinfoil, free from holes, is to be cut to the same size as the glass and laid upon a couple of sheets of filtering or blotting paper folded into quarters. A little mercury is to be placed on the foil, and rubbed over it with a hare's foot, or with a ball of cotton slightly greased with tallow, until the whole of the upper surface of the leaf be amalgamated and bright. More mercury is then to be added, until the quantity is such as to float over the tinfoil. A piece of clean writing paper, with smooth edges, is to be laid upon the mercury, and then the glass surface, previously well cleaned, is to be applied to the paper. The paper is to be drawn out from between the mercury and the glass, while a slight but steady pressure is to be applied to the latter. As the paper recedes it carries all air and dirt with it from between the glass and the metal, which come into perfect contact.

The mirror is now made, and may be used for an experiment; but there is still much more mercury present than is required to make the definite and hard amalgam of tin constituting the usual reflecting surface. If it be desired to remove this excess, the newly-formed mirror must be put under the pressure of a flat board, in a slightly-inclined position, and loaded with weights.

The success of this operation will be found to depend chiefly upon the care exercised in cleaning the glass.

Silvering Glass Mirrors for Optical Purposes.—This is best effected by depositing pure silver on the glass. The light reflected from a mirror made thus has somewhat of a yellowish tinge, but photometric experiments show that from 25 to 30 per cent. more light is reflected than from the old mercurial mirrors.

Where *ammonium aldehyde* can be obtained, there is no doubt that this is the best and most economical process, whether used on a large or a small scale. But those who have not had considerable experience in the laboratory cannot always prepare this compound.

The next best process is based upon the reduction of metallic silver from its ammoniacal solution by salts of tartar. After a trial of several formulæ of this kind, all of them more or less simple, as well as efficacious, the following has been found to yield the best results in the shortest time.

Silvering Solution.—In 1 ounce of distilled or pure rain water, dissolve 48 grains of crystalized nitrate of silver. Precipitate by adding strongest water of ammonia, and continue to add the ammonia drop by drop, stirring the solution with a glass rod, until the brown precipitate is nearly, but not quite redissolved. Filter, and add distilled water to make 12 fluid drachms.

Reducing Solution.—Dissolve in 1 ounce of distilled or very clean rain water, 12 grains of potassium and sodium tartrate (Rochelle or Seignette salts). Boil, in a flask, and while boiling add 2 grains crystalized nitrate of silver dissolved in 1 drachm of water. Continue the boiling five or six minutes. Let cool, filter, and add distilled water to make 12 fluid drachms.

To Silver.—Provision must be made for supporting the glass in a perfectly horizontal position at the surface of the liquid. This is best done by cementing to the face of the mirror three nice hooks by which it may be hung from a temporary framework—easily made out of a few sticks.

The glass to be silvered must be cleansed by immersing it in strong nitric acid, washing in liquor potassæ, and thoroughly rinsing with distilled water. If the glass has had mercurial amalgam on it, it will probably be necessary to clean the back with rouge. On having this surface perfectly, chemically clean, depends in a great measure the success of the operation.

Having arranged the contrivance for suspending the glass

so that it may be at exactly the right height in the vessel that is to receive the solution, remove this vessel and pour into it enough of equal quantities of the two solutions to fill it exactly to the previously ascertained level. Stir the solutions so that they will become thoroughly mixed, and replace the glass to be silvered, taking great care that the surface to be silvered shall come in contact with the silvering fluid exactly at all points. The glass plate should be rinsed carefully before replacing, and should be put in while wet. Great care should be taken that no air bubbles remain on the surface of the solution, or between it and the surface to be silvered.

Now set the vessel in the sun for a few minutes, if the weather be warm, or by the fire, if it be cold, as a temperature of 45° to 50° C. (113° to 122° Fah.) is most conducive to the rapid deposition of a brilliant, firm and even film of silver. The fluid in the sunlight soon becomes inky black, gradually clearing as the silver is reduced, until when exhausted it is perfectly clear. The mirror should be removed before this point is reached, as a process of bleaching sets up if left after the fluid is exhausted. From 20 to 80 minutes, according to the weather, purity of chemicals, etc., is required for the entire process.

When the mirror is removed from the bath, it should be carefully rinsed with distilled water from the wash bottle, and laid on its edge on blotting paper to dry. When perfectly dry, the back should be varnished with some elastic varnish and allowed to dry. The wires and cement can now be removed from the face, and the glass cleaned with a little fledget of cotton and a minute drop of nitric acid, taking great care that the acid does not get to the edges or under the varnish. Rinse, dry and the mirror is finished.

Silver Amalgam for Mirrors.—The great objections to mirrors coated with pure silver are the yellow character of the reflected light, and the fact that such mirrors are apt to be affected by sulphur. M. Lenoir has invented a process which is said to avoid these difficulties. The glass is first silvered by means of tartaric acid and ammoniacal nitrate of silver, or by the process described in the preceding section, and is then exposed to the action of a weak solution of double cyanide of mercury and potassium. When the mercurial solution has spread uniformly over the surface, fine zinc dust is powdered over it, which promptly reduces the quicksilver, and permits it to form a white and brilliant silver amalgam, adhering strongly to the glass, and which is affirmed to be free from the yellowish tint of ordinary silvered glass, and not easily affected by sulphurous emanations.

Care of Looking Glasses.—When looking glasses are exposed to the direct rays of the sun or to very strong heat from a fire the amalgam is apt to crystallize and the mirror loses its brilliancy. If a mirror is placed where the rays of the sun can strike it, it should be covered in that part of the day during which it is exposed.

The best method of cleaning looking glasses is as follows : Take a newspaper, fold it small, dip it into a basin of clean cold water. When thoroughly wet squeeze it out as you do a sponge ; then rub it pretty hard all over the surface of the glass, taking care that it is not so wet as to run down in streams ; in fact, the paper must only be completely moistened or dampened all through. Let it rest a few minutes, then go over the glass with a piece of fresh newspaper till it looks clear and bright. The insides of windows may be cleaned in the same way; also spectacle-glasses, lamp-glasses, etc. White paper that has not been printed on is better; but in the absence of that, a very old newspaper, on which the ink has become thoroughly dried, should be used. Writing paper will not answer.

Nickel.

This is by far the most valuable metal that has been brought into notice during the past few years. It has been long familiar to chemists, and as a component of German silver, electrum, and similar alloys, it has been in common use, but as an unalloyed coating for other metals it has only been employed for about ten years.

It is hard, not easily corroded by acids, and, unlike silver, it is entirely unaffected by sulphur. In addition to these valuable qualities it has one of special importance in some cases, and that is the ease with which a nickel surface slides over any other smooth body. Hence, for the sliding parts of telescopes, microscopes, etc., it has come into very general use, and it is not improbable that it will prove of great value in the case of slide valves, pistons, etc.

Nickel is almost always applied as a coating by the electroplating process, for instructions in which art we must refer our readers to any good work on the art of electro-metallurgy.

A foreign journal gives the following directions for nickel plating without a battery : To a solution of five to ten per cent. of chloride of zinc, as pure as possible, add sufficient sulphate of nickel to produce a strong green color, and bring to boiling in a porcelain vessel. The piece to be plated, which must be perfectly bright and free from grease, is introduced so that it touches the vessel as little as possible. Ebullition is continued from 30 to 60 minutes, water being added from time to time to replace that evaporated. During ebullition nickel is precipitated in the form of a white and brilliant coating. The boiling can be continued for hours without sensibly increasing the thickness of this coating. As soon as the object appears to be plated it is washed in water containing a little chalk in suspension, and then carefully dried. This coating may be scoured with chalk, and is very adherent. The chloride of zinc and also the sulphate of nickel used must be free from metals precipitable by iron. If during the precipitation the liquor becomes colorless, sulphate of nickel should be added. The spent liquor may be used again by exposing to the air until the contained iron is precipitated, filtering and adding the zinc and nickel salts as above. Cobalt also may be deposited in the same manner.

Noise—Prevention of.

To those who carry on any operations requiring much hammering or pounding, a simple means of deadening the noise of their work is a great relief. Several methods have been suggested, but the best are probably these :

1. Rubber cushions under the legs of the work-bench. *Chamber's Journal* describes a factory where the hammering of fifty coppersmiths was scarcely audible in the room below, their benches having under each leg a rubber cushion.

2. Kegs of sand or sawdust applied in the same way. A few inches of sand or sawdust is first poured into each keg; on this is laid a board or block upon which the leg rests, and round the leg and block is poured fine dry sand or sawdust. Not only all noise, but all vibration and shock, is prevented ; and an ordinary anvil, so mounted, may be used in a dwelling house without annoying the inhabitants. To amateurs, whose workshops are almost always located in

dwelling houses, this device affords a cheap and simple relief from a very great annoyance.

Painting Bright Metals.

When paint is applied to bright metals like tin or zinc, it is very apt to peel off. This difficulty is greatly lessened if the metal be hot when the paint is applied, but in many cases this cannot be done. In such cases the surface of the metal should be corroded, for which purpose a solution of sulphate of copper, acidulated with nitric acid answers well. The metal should be washed with the solution, allowed to stand a couple of hours, and then washed with clean water and dried.

Painting the Hours on Metal Dials.—The black coloring matter is the soot obtained by holding a clean copper or sheet metal plate over the flame of an oil or petroleum lamp (a glowing tool serves the purpose very well). As soon as a sufficient deposit is produced it is collected on a piece of glass, care being taken not to mix any foreign substance with it. A few drops of essence of lavender are then poured on the soot and the mixture pounded with a spatula. This done, just sufficient copal varnish is added to give the composition a proper thickness, so as to prevent it spreading when applied. The varnish thus prepared is put on by means of a very fine brush. To secure brilliancy the dial is dried at a slow heat, by passing it lightly over a spirit flame, the reverse side of the dial being, of course, the only part exposed to the flame. This composition must be made in quantities large enough for present use only, as it dries very rapidly and cannot be utilized afterwards. To secure good results this process requires some experience, which can only be obtained by careful experiments. The painting especially requires a certain aptitude and lightness of hand, which may, however, soon be attained by strict attention.

This process, which gives very excellent results, is evidently applicable to a great variety of purposes.

Paper.

There are so many purposes to which paper is applied that a small volume might be filled with a description of them. The following are those which will probably prove most useful to the amateur :

Adhesive Paper.—Paper in sheets, half of which are

gummed on both sides, and the other half on one side, and divided into strips and squares of different sizes by perforations, like sheets of postage stamps, are very convenient in many ways—the doubly-gummed answering for fixing drawings in books, labels on glass, etc. It is stated that the mixture by which it is coated is prepared by dissolving six parts of glue, previously soaked for a day in cold water, two parts of sugar, and three parts of gum arabic, in twenty-four parts of water, by the aid of heat.

Barometer Paper.—This is paper impregnated with a so-called sympathetic ink, which alters its color by a change of temperature. The most delicate substance to accomplish this is *sulphocyanide of cobalt*, originally proposed by Grotthus. This is prepared by adding an alcoholic solution of potassium sulphocyanide to an aqueous solution of cobaltous sulphate, until no more potassium sulphate separates. The whole is transferred to a filter, and the residue on the filter (potassium sulphate) washed with alcohol. The dilute filtrate may be used as it is, for impregnating paper, or it may be concentrated by very careful evaporation at as low a temperature as possible. The salt may be obtained crystalline by removing the alcoholic menstruum in the vacuum of an air-pump. It forms violet columns, soluble in water with red color. Paper impregnated with the *alcoholic* solution, or on which tracings have been made with the latter, turns reddish in *dry* air, but assumes a *blue* color at the slightest elevation of temperature.

Creases, To Take out of Drawing Paper or Engravings.—Lay the paper or engraving, face downwards, on a sheet of smooth, unsized white paper ; cover it with another sheet of the same, very slightly damped, and iron with a moderately warm flat iron.

Drawing Paper, To Mount.—Sometimes it is difficult to get a drawing on a sheet of paper of the ordinary sizes when stretched upon a board, by reason of the waste edges used to secure the paper firmly ; and again, in stiff papers, such as the "Eggshell," so called, ordinary mucilage does not possess sufficient strength, and glue has to be substituted, to the annoyance of the draughtsman. The following is a very simple way of obviating these difficulties : First moisten the paper thoroughly ; then lay it upon the board in proper position, and, with blotting paper, remove most of the moisture for a distance of half an inch or thereabouts from the edges; then take strips of Manila paper (not too stiff) about one and a half inches wide, covered on one side with mucilage, and paste them down on both paper and board, allowing them to lap on the edges of the sheet about half an inch. Keep the middle of the sheet thoroughly wet until the mucilage on the edges has set, when the whole sheet may be allowed to dry gradually. It will be found that this method is quicker and surer than any other, and is of great use where it is necessary to color on mounted paper.

Glass-Paper.—Paper coated with glass is known by this name just as paper coated with fine sharp sand is called *sandpaper*, and paper coated with emery is called *emery paper*. Paper or a cheap cloth is coated with thinnish glue, dusted heavily and evenly with glass-powder of the proper fineness, and allowed to become nearly dry. The superfluous powder is then shaken off, the sheets are pressed to make them even, and afterwards thoroughly dried.

The objection to ordinary glass-paper is that it is easily injured by heat and moisture. If the glue be mixed with a little bichromate of potassa before it is applied to the cloth, and exposed for some time to strong bright sunshine while it is drying, it will become insoluble in water.

The glue may also be rendered insoluble by the process of tanning. The paper or cloth is first soaked in a solution of tannic acid and dried. The glue is then applied, the powdered glass dusted on, and over it is dusted a little tannic acid. If the glue be not very moist, it should be damped by means of an atomiser, a very cheap form of which is figured in *The Young Scientist*, vol. 2. The sheets are then slowly dried and will be found to resist moisture very thoroughly.

Paper, To Prepare for Varnishing.—To prevent the absorption of varnish, and injury to any color or design on the paper, it is necessary to first give it two or three coats of size. The best size for white or delicate colors is made by dissolving a little isinglass in boiling water, or by boiling some clean parchment cuttings until they form a clear solution; then strain through a piece of clean muslin. It may be applied with a clean soft paint brush, the first coat, especially, very lightly. The best brush for this purpose is the kind used by varnishers for giving the finishing flow coats of varnish, wide, flat and soft; or where there is much danger of injuring a design, and the paper article will allow of it, it is a good plan for the first coat, to pour the solution into a wide, flat dish, and pass the paper through it once, and back again, and then hang it up to dry. For less delicate purposes, a little light-colored glue, soaked over night in enough water to cover it, and then dissolved by heat, adding hot water enough to dilute it sufficiently, will make an excellent sizing.

Pollen Powder, or Paper Powder.—Boil white paper or paper cuttings in water for five hours. Pour off the water, pound the pulp in a wedgwood mortar, and pass through a fine sieve. This powder is employed by the bird stuffers to dust over the legs of some birds, and the bills of others, to give them a powdery appearance; also to communicate the downy bloom to rough-coated artificial fruit, and other purposes of a similar nature; it makes excellent pounce.

Tracing Paper.—Tracing paper may be purchased so cheaply that it is hardly worth while to make it; and there is a very fine, tough kind now in market which may be mounted and colored almost like drawing paper. Those who desire to prepare some for themselves will find that the following directions give a good result. The inventor of the process received a medal and premium from the Society of Arts for it.

Open a quire of tough tissue paper, and brush the first sheet with a mixture of equal parts of mastic varnish and oil of turpentine. Proceed with each sheet similarly and dry them on lines by hanging them up singly. As the process goes on, the under sheets absorb a portion of the varnish, and require less than if single sheets were brushed separately. The paper, when dry, is quite light and transparent, and may readily be written on with ink.

Transfer paper.—This is useful for copying patterns, drawings, etc. Designs for scroll saws may be copied very neatly by means of it. It is easily made by rubbing a thin but tough unglazed paper with a mixture of lard and lampblack. The copy is made by laying a sheet of the transfer or, as it is sometimes called, *manifold* paper, over a clean sheet of drawing or writing paper, and over it the drawing to be copied. The lines of the drawing are then carefully traced with a fine but blunt point, and the pressure along the lines transfers to the clean paper underneath a perfect copy. To keep the under side of the drawing or pattern clean, a sheet of tissue paper may be placed between it and the transfer paper.

Water Stains, To Remove from Engravings or Paper.—Fill a large vessel with pure water and dip the engraving in, waving it backward and forward until thoroughly wet. Then spread a sheet of clean white paper on a drawing board, lay the engraving on it and fasten both to the board with drawing pins. Expose it to bright sunshine, keeping it moist until the stains disappear, which will not be long. This is simply a modification of the old system of bleaching linen.

Waxed Paper.—Paper saturated with wax, paraffin or stearin is very useful for wrapping up articles which should be kept dry and not exposed to the air. Place a sheet of stout paper on a heated iron plate, and over this place the sheets of unglazed paper—tissue paper does very well—that are to be waxed. Enclose the wax or paraffin in a piece of muslin, and as it melts spread it evenly over the paper.

Patina.

An imitation of patina for bronze objects of all kinds can be produced by preparing a paint of carbonate of copper and any light alcoholic varnish, and applying it to the object with a brush. This green color penetrates the smallest recesses, and has, when dry, the appearance of patina. Carbonate of copper gives a blue patina, verdigris a light green, and intermediate shades of color can be obtained by mixing the two.

Patterns—To Trace.

There are various methods of making copies of patterns on paper, the simplest perhaps being the use of the tracing paper described on another page.

When a few duplicates of patterns for embroidery are required, they may be very easily made by hand as follows :

The drawing is made upon paper; then lay the drawing upon an even cloth, and perforate all the lines with a fine needle, close and even. Then take finely powdered charcoal, three parts, resin one part in fine powder; mix and tie it in a piece of porous calico, so that it forms a dusting bag. Lay the perforated drawing upon your material, hold down with one hand, rub the dusting-bag over the drawing; the dust will fall through the holes and form the drawing on the material. Remove the paper drawing, lay blotting-paper over the dust pattern, and go over it with a warm flat iron The heat will melt the resin and fix the drawing on the material.

Pencils as a Substitute for Ink.

Aniline pencils have been in use for some time, and have given good satisfaction, but the following is said to give even better results. Pencils made after the following formula give a very black writing, capable of being reproduced by the copying machine, and which does not fade on exposure to light. The mass for these pencils is prepared as follows: 10 pounds of the best logwood are repeatedly boiled in 10 gallons of water, straining each time. The liquid is then evaporated down till it weighs 10 pounds, and is then allowed to boil in a pan of stoneware or enamel. To the boiling liquid, nitrate of oxide of chrome is added in small quantities, until the bronze-colored precipitate formed at first is redissolved with a deep blue coloration. This solution is then evaporated in the water bath down to a sirup, with which is mixed well kneaded clay in the proportion of 1 part of clay to $3\frac{1}{2}$ of extract. A little gum tragacanth is also added to obtain a proper consistence.

It is absolutely necessary to use the salt of chrome in the right proportion. An excess of this salt gives a disagreeable appearance to the writing, while if too little is used the black matter is not sufficiently soluble.

The other salts of chrome cannot be used in this preparation, as they would crystallize, and the writing would scale off as it dried.

The nitrate of oxide of chrome is prepared by precipitating a hot solution of chrome alum with a suitable quantity of carbonate of soda. The precipitate is washed till the filtrate is free from sulphuric acid. The precipitate thus obtained is dissolved in pure nitric acid, so as to leave a little still undissolved. Hence the solution contains no free acid, which would give the ink a dirty red color. Oxalic acid and caustic alkalies do not attack the writing. Dilute nitric acid reddens, but does not obliterate the characters.

Pencil Marks—To Fix.

To fix Pencil Marks so they will not rub out, take well-skimmed milk and dilute with an equal bulk of water. Wash the pencil marks (whether writing or drawing) with this liquid, using a soft, flat camel-hair brush, and avoiding all rubbing. Place upon a flat board to dry.

Pewter.

The principal constituents of pewter are lead and tin; the proportions of the two metals depending somewhat on the use to which the alloy is put. The best contains but 16 to 20 per cent. of lead. Of this plates and dishes are made, which look like block tin, and can be brightly polished by rubbing. The addition of more lead cheapens the commodity, and gives it a dull bluish appearance. In France pewter vessels for wine and vinegar contain 18 per cent. of lead. It has been found that a larger proportion of that metal in utensils for this purpose is liable to result in the formation, in the liquid, of the poisonous acetate or sugar of lead.

A little copper added in making pewter hardens the compound and renders it sonorous, so that toy trumpets and other rude musical instruments can be made of it. If the copper is replaced by antimony, hardness and a silvery lustre are the result. If the contents of the melting pot are stirred with a strip half of zinc and half of tin, or if a lump of zinc is allowed to float on the melted metal during the casting, the vaporized spelter seems to protect the fluid mass from oxidation, and prevents the formation of dross. Hence it is said to " cleanse " the mass.

Jewellers use polishers and laps of pewter, and sheets of the article are to some extent used for cheap engraving, music notes, or other figures being stamped upon it instead of being cut with a burin or graver. The ease with which it melts causes it to be employed by tinsmiths and tinkers for solder. Care must be taken not to set pewter dishes, mugs, spoons, lamps, etc., on stoves or other hot bodies, as, if left for any time, they are liable to settle into shapeless lumps.

Pillows for the Sick Room.

Save all your scraps of writing paper, old envelopes, old notes of no use for keeping, old backs of notes, etc. Cut them in strips about one-half inch wide and two inches long, and curl them well with an old penknife. Make a pillow case of any materials you have; fill it with your curled paper mixed with a few shreds of flannel. Stuff it quite full, sew up the end and cover as you please, These pillows are invaluable in cases of fever, as they keep constantly cool and allow a circulation of air.

Plaster of Paris.

Plaster of Paris is a well known material, obtained by exposing the purer varieties of gypsum or alabaster to a heat a little above that of boiling water, when it becomes a fine, white dry powder. Sometimes the gypsum is first reduced to a fine powder and then heated in iron pans, and in this case the operation is sometimes called "boiling" plaster, because the escape of the water, with which crystalline gypsum is always combined, gives to the fine powder the appearance of *boiling*. Plaster of Paris, after being boiled, rapidly deteriorates when exposed to the air, consequently when plaster is required for making cements or for other purposes for which a good article is needed, care must be taken to secure that which is good and freshly boiled. The Italian image makers always use a superior quality of plaster, and it may generally be obtained from them in small quantity.

The employment of gypsum in casting, and in all cases where impressions are required, is very extensive. A thin pulp of 1 part gypsum and 2½ parts water is made; this pulp hardens by standing. The hardening of good, well-burnt gypsum is effected in one to two minutes, and more quickly in a moderate heat. Models are made in this substance for galvano-plastic purposes, for metallic castings, and for ground works in porcelain manufacture. The object from which the cast is to be taken is first well oiled to prevent the adhesion of the gypsum. When greater hardness is required a small quantity of lime is added; this addition gives a very marble-like appearance, and the mixture is much employed in architecture, being then known as gypsum-marble or stucco. The gypsum is generally mixed with lime water, to which sometimes a solution of sulphate of zinc is added. After drying, the surface is rubbed down with pumice stone, colored to represent marble, and polished with Tripoli and olive oil. Artificial scagliola work is largely composed of gypsum.

There are several methods of hardening gypsum. One of the oldest consists in mixing the burnt gypsum with limewater or a solution of gum arabic. Another, yielding very good results, is to mix the gypsum with a solution of 20 ounces of alum in 6 pounds of water; this plaster hardens completely in 15 to 30 minutes, and is largely used under the name of marble cement. Parian cement is gypsum hardened by means of borax, 1 part borax being dissolved in 9 parts of water, and the gypsum treated with the solution. Still better results are obtained by the addition to this solution of 1 part of cream of tartar.

The hardening of gypsum with a water-glass solution is found difficult, and no better results are obtained than with ordinary gypsum. Fissot obtains artificial stone from gypsum by burning and immersions in water, first for half a minute, after which it is exposed to the air and again for two to three minutes, when the block appears as a hardened stone. It would seem from this method that the augmentation in hardness is due to a new crystalization. Hardened gypsum, treated with stearic acid or with paraffine, and polished, much resembles meerschaum; the resemblance may be increased by a coloring solution of gamboge and dragon's blood, to impart a faint red-yellow tint. The cheap artificial meerschaum pipes are manufactured by this method.

Poisons.

Many of the substances used in the arts are highly poisonous. Indeed, some of the most virulent poisons are employed in very common operations. Thus arsenic is used for coloring brass; the strong acids are used in every machine shop and foundry, and even prussic acid may be occasionally produced during the employment of prussiate of potash. The extremely poisonous cyanide of potassium is used by every photographer and electroplater. Even into the household, poisons too frequently find their way. Our matches are tipped with a strong poison, and housekeepers are often too ready with poison for the destruction of vermin. Phosphorous, arsenic and corrosive sublimate, are too frequently thus used. Paris green also we have actually seen used for the destruction of cockroaches in pantries, and corrosive sublimate is in common use as a poison for bed-bugs. As a bug poison it is generally dissolved in alcohol or whiskey, and the odor and taste have sometimes proved a strong temptation to persons who did not fully realize its dangerous character. All bottles containing such mixtures should therefore be carefully labelled, "POISON," in large letters, and when emptied they should either be broken, or very carefully cleansed, since accidents have arisen from careless persons pouring drinkable liquids into bottles that have contained solutions of corrosive sublimate, which solutions, after drying up have left the bottle apparently empty, but in reality containing an amount of poison sufficient to destroy several lives.

In all cases where poisons have been swallowed, the proper course is first to neutralize the deleterious agent, and then to procure its rejection by means either of the stomach-pump or an emetic. The stomach-pump is, of course, the best and most expeditious agent. It requires but a few moments to insert it and remove the contents of the stomach; fresh supplies of water and the proper antidotes can then be poured into the organ, so that in a few minutes the last traces of the poison can be removed. But as the stomach-pump is to be found in the possession of physicians only, reliance must in general be placed upon emetics, of which the best is, unquestionably, mustard—an article which is to be found in almost every household. It is generally conceded by physicians that mustard is the mildest, most rapid, and most efficient emetic known. It is prepared for use as follows: Take about a plump dessert-spoonful of genuine flour of mustard (if it be mixed with wheat flour or turmeric, more will be needed), and mix it rapidly in a cup with water to the consistency of thin gruel, and let this be swallowed without delay or hesitation. In a very few seconds the contents of the stomach will be ejected. Before the emetic action has entirely ceased, a little lukewarm water, or still better, warm milk, should be forced down. This will be thrown off immediately, and will serve to rinse out the stomach and remove the last traces of deleterious matter.

By the time the operation of the emetic has ceased, a physician will probably be in attendance, and to his care the patient should be at once confided.

The following notes on special poisons will prove useful:

Strong Acid.—Where nitric, sulphuric or hydrochloric acid has been swallowed, it is well to administer carbonate of soda before giving the emetic.

Oxalic Acid.—This acid is often found among the articles provided for household use, being used for cleaning brass and various metals, as well as for removing stains of ink and iron mould. In former times it was used for cleaning boot tops and for some other purposes. In appearance it resembles epsom salts so closely that even experienced chemists might be deceived, if it were not for the taste, for while the acid is intensely sour the salts are as intensely bitter.

The proper antidote to oxalic acid is some form of lime, and the best method of administering it is to mix finely pulverized chalk with water to the consistency of cream and swallow it. It is a singular fact that when oxalic acid is largely diluted with water, it acts very rapidly and energetically, destroying life almost with the rapidity of prussic acid. Hence to administer soapy water, or any other very diluted remedy, would be almost fatal. And yet this course was actually recommended by a popular scientific journal.

Prussic Acid.—As this is one of the most rapid of all poisons in its action, prompt and energetic measures are demanded. Cold affusion to the head and spine has been found the most efficacious mode of treatment. Internal remedies appear to be of no service. The vapor of ammonia may be cautiously applied to the nostrils, and stimulating liniments by friction to the chest and abdomen, but unless the dose is small, and the patient is seen early, there can be little hope of benefit from any treatment. Certain chemical substances (cyanides) from which prussic acid is slowly evolved by the action of the air, are used in electro-plating and in photography. These substances are themselves very strong poisons, and if accidentally swallowed they cause death with such rapidity that there is scarcely any time to apply any remedies. Green copperas (sulphate of iron) dissolved in water and administered would decompose and neutralize the poison, after which the directions given for prussic acid should be followed. When poisoning occurs from breathing the vapors arising from these salts, it is caused by prussic acid, and should be treated accordingly.

Arsenic—Paris Green.—By *arsenic* is generally meant the white oxide of the metal arsenic. It is also known as *arsenious* acid. Paris green is well known and owes its deadly properties to arsenic. In all cases in which poisonous doses of arsenic have been swallowed, our great dependance must be placed upon emetics and purgatives. Persons who take arsenic upon a full stomach frequently escape its effects, and therefore it is always well to give copious draughts of milk, or, if more convenient, raw eggs, beaten up. Then, as soon as possible, administer an emetic (mustard is as good as any) and keep up its action by giving milk during the intervals of the paroxysms of vomiting. When the stomach no longer rejects what is swallowed, give a good dose of castor oil.

Corrosive Sublimate.—When corrosive sublimate has been swallowed, the first thing to be done is, if possible, to get rid of it, either by means of emetics or the stomach-pump. If the poison has been taken on a full stomach, an emetic or the pump is the first thing in order; if the stomach be empty, it will be better to administer, in the first place, as much white of egg, or milk, or mixture of both, as the patient can be made to swallow, and immediately afterwards give an emetic. The white of eggs is the great antidote for corrosive sublimate, but it is of no use where the poison has been absorbed into the system, and if, after administering white of eggs, we neglect to procure its rejection, the compound that is formed may be destroyed by the action of the gastric juice, and left free to act with all its original virulence.

Phosphorous.—There is no efficient antidote or remedy for poisoning by phosphorous. Taylor recommends the administration of emetics, and of albuminous or mucilaginous drinks, holding hydrate of magnesia suspended. The exhibition of oil would be decidedly injurious, as this dissolves and tends to diffuse the poison. Saline purgatives should therefore be preferred.

Opium.—When a poisonous dose of opium has been taken, the first object should be to remove the poison, and this must frequently be accomplished by the stomach-pump, as emetics are of little service when the patient has lost the power of swallowing. Dashing cold water on the head, chest, and spine, has been adopted with great success; in the treatment of infants, the plunging of the body into a warm bath, and suddenly removing it from the water into the cold air, has been found a most effectual method of rousing them. Severe whipping on the palms of the hands and soles of the feet or the back has also been successfully employed. A common plan for rousing an adult is to keep him in continual motion, by making him walk between two assistants. Above all things, the tendency to fall into a state of lethargy must be prevented. A strong decoction of coffee has been frequently employed as a stimulant to promote recovery, and apparently with benefit.

Strychnine.—When this poison has been absorbed and conveyed into the blood there is no known antidote to its action. But if spasms have not already set in so as to close the jaws, we should, by the stomach-pump or by emetics, endeavor to remove the poison. In a case in which six grains of strychnine were taken, the life of the person appears to have been saved by the early use of the stomach-pump. It has been supposed that emetics would not act in these cases; but this is an error based on imperfect observation. In one case a man took three grains of strychnine, dissolved in rectified spirits and diluted sulphuric acid. He went to bed and slept for about an hour and a half, when he awoke in a spasm, uttering loud cries, which alarmed the household. Free vomiting was brought on by the use of emetics, and this, combined with other treatment, led to his recovery. The first step, therefore, in every case, should be to induce vomiting.

Ivy Poisoning.—The best remedy for ivy poisoning is said to be sweet spirits of nitre. Bathe the parts affected freely with this fluid three or four times during the day, and the next morning scarcely any trace of poison will be found. If the blisters be broken, so as to allow the spirits to penetrate the cuticle, a single application will be sufficient.

Stings.—Extract the sting, which is always left behind by bees, and bathe the parts with cold water, or apply a good poultice of common clay mud. Liquid ammonia mixed either with the water or the mud, will prove of service. All liniments which require rubbing are bad, as tending to irritate the part and diffuse the poison. Above all, avoid scratching the wound.

Polishing Powders.

Nothing is more necessary to the successful use of polishing powder than *equality* in the grain. Fine dust clogs the action of coarse grinding powders, and prevents them from cutting with rapidity the object to be ground; coarse particles mixed with fine polishing powder scratch the article to be polished, and render grinding and polishing necessary again. To secure fineness and uniformity no process equals that of elutriation, which is thus performed: Suppose it were desired to separate the ordinary flour of emery into three different degrees of fineness. Take three vessels (such as tin pails or glass jars) and mix the emery with a large quantity of water—say a quart of water to 1½ oz. of emery. Stir the mixture until the emery is thoroughly diffused through the liquid, and allow to stand five minutes. By this time all the heavier particles will have settled, and on pouring the fluid into a second jar only the finer portion will be carried over. So continue to wash the first residuum until nearly all the particles have subsided at the end of five minutes, and the water is left comparatively clear. You will now have the coarse portion, No. 1, by itself.

So, from the sediment collected from the washings of No. 1, you may collect a portion, No. 2, having a second degree of coarseness. The last and finest will be obtained by letting the final washings stand ten or fifteen minutes, pouring off the liquid and allowing it to settle.

The principal polishing powders are chalk or whiting, crocus or rouge, emery, oilstone powder, and putty or tutty, which latter consists chiefly of oxide of tin. Other powders, such as tripoli, bath-brick, sand, etc., are rarely used for the finer kinds of work. Emery is so well known that it does not need description.

Chalk or Whiting.—Chalk is a native carbonate of lime, consisting of the remains of minute creatures known as *foraminifera*, and when simply scraped or crushed under a hammer or runner, it is sometimes used for polishing such soft substances as bone, ivory, etc. As it contains particles of silica of varying size, it cuts freely, but is apt to scratch. To remove the gritty particles, the chalk is ground, and the finer parts separated by washing. It then becomes *whiting*, which is generally sold in lumps. Whiting has very poor cutting qualities, and it is therefore used chiefly as *plate powder* for cleaning gold, silver, glass, etc., and for absorbing grease from metals which have been polished by other means.

Prepared Chalk.—This is a manufactured article, prepared by adding a solution of carbonate of soda to a solution of chloride of calcium (both cheap salts), so long as a precipitate is thrown down. The solutions should be carefully filtered through paper before being mixed, and dust should be rigorously excluded. The white powder which falls down is carbonate of lime, or chalk, and when carefully washed and dried, it forms a most excellent polishing powder for the softer metals. The particles are almost impalpable, but seem to be crystalline, for they polish quickly and smoothly, though they seem to wear away the material so little that its form or sharpness is not injured to any perceptible degree.

Crocus or Rouge.—These articles are manufactured at Liverpool, by persons who make it their sole occupation, in the following manner :

They take crystals of sulphate of iron (green vitriol or copperas), immediately from the crystallizing vessels, in the copperas works there, so as to have them as clean as possible; and instantly put them into crucibles or cast iron pots, and expose them to heat, without suffering the smallest particle of dust to get in, which would have a tendency to scratch the articles to be polished. Those portions which are least calcined and are of a scarlet color, are fit to make rouge for polishing gold or silver, while those which are calcined or have become red-purple or bluish-purple, form crocus fit for polishing brass or steel. Of these, the bluish-purple colored parts are the hardest, and are found nearest to the bottom of the vessels, and consequently have been exposed to the greatest degree of heat.

Mr. Andrew Ross's mode of preparing Oxide of Iron.— Dissolve crystals of sulphate of iron in water; filter the solution to separate some particles of silex which are generally present, and sometimes are abundant; then precipitate from this filtered solution the protoxide of iron, by the addition of a saturated solution of soda, which must also be filtered. This grey oxide is to be repeatedly washed and then dried; put it in this state into a crucible, and very gradually raise it to a dull red heat; then pour it into a clean metal or earthen dish, and while cooling it will absorb oxygen from the atmosphere, and acquire a beautiful dark red color. In this state it is fit for polishing the softer metals, as silver and gold, but will scarcely make any impression on hardened steel or glass. For these latter purposes I discovered that it is the black oxide that affected the polish (and this gives to the red oxide a purple hue, which is used as the criterion of its cutting quality in ordinary), therefore for polishing the harder materials the oxide must be heated to a bright red, and kept in that state until a sufficient quantity of it is converted into black oxide to give the mass a deep purple hue when exposed to the atmosphere. I have converted the whole into black oxide; but this is liable to scratch, and does not work so pleasantly as when mixed with the softer material. The powder must now be levigated with a soft wrought iron spatula, upon a soft iron slab, and afterwards washed in a very weak solution of gum arabic, as recommended by Dr. Green in his paper on specula. The oxide prepared in this manner is almost impalpable, and free from all extraneous matter, and has the requisite quality in an eminent degree for polishing steel, glass, the softer gems, etc.

Lord Ross's Mode of preparing the Peroxide of Iron.— "I prepare the peroxide of iron by precipitation with water of ammonia from a pure dilute solution of sulphate of iron; the precipitate is washed, pressed in a screw press till nearly dry, and exposed to a heat which in the dark appears a dull low red. The only points of importance are, that the sulphate of iron should be pure, that the water of ammonia should be decidedly in excess, and that the heat should not exceed that I have described. The color will be a bright crimson inclining to yellow. I have tried both soda and potash, pure, instead of water of ammonia, but after washing with some degree of care, a trace of the alkali still remained, and the peroxide was of an ochrey color till overheated, and did not polish properly."

Oilstone Powder.—The Turkey oilstone can hardly be considered as a hone slate, having nothing of a lamellar or schistose appearance. As a whetstone it surpasses every other known substance, and possesses, in an eminent degree, the property of abrading the hardest steel, and is, at the same time, of so compact and close a nature as to resist the pressure necessary for sharpening a graver or other small instrument of that description. Little more is known of its natural history than that it is found in the interior of Asia Minor, and brought down to Smyrna for sale. The white and black varieties of Turkey oilstone differ but little in their general characters; the black is, however, somewhat harder, and is imported in larger pieces than the white.

Fragments of oilstone, when pulverized, sifted and washed, are much in request by mechanicians. This abrasive is generally preferred for grinding together those fittings of mathematical instruments and machinery, which are made wholly or in part of brass or gun metal, for oilstone being softer and more pulverulent than emery, is less liable to become embedded in the metal than emery, which latter is then apt continually to grind, and ultimately damage the accuracy of the fittings of brass works. In modern practice it is usual, however, as far as possible, to discard the grinding together of surfaces, with the view of producing accuracy of form, or precision of contact.

Oilstone powder is preferred to pumice-stone powder for polishing superior brass works, and it is also used by the watchmaker on rubbers of pewter in polishing steel.

Pumice-stone Powder.—Pumice-stone is a volcanic product, and is obtained principally from the Campo Bianco, one of the Lipari islands, which is entirely composed of this substance. It is extensively employed in various branches of the arts, and particularly in the state of powder, for polishing the various articles of cut glass; it is also extensively used in dressing leather, and in grinding and polishing the surface of metallic plates, etc.

Pumice-stone is ground or crushed under a runner, and sifted, and in this state it is used for brass and other metal works, and also for japanned, varnished and painted goods, for which latter purposes it is generally applied on woolen cloths with water.

Putty Powder is the pulverized oxide of tin, or generally of tin and lead mixed in various proportions. The process of manufacture is alike in all cases—the metal is oxidized in an iron muffle, or a rectangular box, close on all sides, except a square hole in the front side. The retort is surrounded by fire, and kept at a red heat, so that its contents are partially ignited, and they are continually stirred to expose fresh portions to the heated air; the process is complete when the fluid metal entirely disappears, and the upper part of the oxide then produced, sparkles somewhat like particles of incandescent charcoal. The oxide is then removed with ladles, and spread over the bottom of large iron cooling pans and allowed to cool. The lumps of oxide which are as hard as marble, are then selected from the mass and ground dry under the runner; the putty powder is afterwards carefully sifted through lawn.

As a criterion of quality it may be said that the whitest putty powder is the purest, provided it be heavy. Some of the common kinds are brown and yellow, while others, from the intentional admixture of a little ivory black, are known as *grey putty*. The pure white putty which is used by marble workers, opticians and some others, is the smoothest and most cutting; it should consist of the oxide of tin alone, but to lessen the difficulty of manufacture, a very little lead (the linings of tea chests), or else an alloy called *shruff* (prepared in ingots by the pewterers) is added to assist the oxidation.

The putty powder of commerce of good fair quality, is made of about equal parts of tin and lead, or tin and shruff; the common dark colored kinds are prepared of lead only, but these are much harsher to the touch, and altogether inferior.

Perhaps the most extensive use of putty powder, is in glass and marble works, but the best kind serves admirably as plate powder, and for the general purposes of polishing.

Putty powder for fine optical purposes is prepared by Mr. A. Ross by the following method, which is the result of many experiments. Metallic tin is dissolved in nitro-muriatic acid, and precipitated from the filtered solution by liquid ammonia, both fluids being largely diluted with water. The peroxide of tin is then washed in abundance of water, collected in a cloth filter, and squeezed as dry as possible in a piece of new clean linen; the mass is now subjected to pressure in a screw-press, or between lever boards, to make it as dry as possible. When the lump thus produced has been broken in pieces and dried in the air, it is finally levigated while dry on a plate of glass with an iron spatula, and afterwards exposed in a crucible to a *low* white heat.

Before the peroxide has been heated, or while it is in the levigated *hydrous* state, the putty powder possesses but little cutting quality, as under the microscope, the particles then appear to have no determined form, or to be *amorphous*, and, on being wetted, to resume the gelatinous condition of the hydrous precipitate, so as to be useless for polishing; whereas, when the powder is heated, to render it *anhydrous*, most of the particles take their natural form, that of *lamellar crystals*, and act with far more energy (yet without scratching) than any of the ordinary polishing powders. The whole mass requires to be washed or elutriated in the usual manner after having been heated, in order to separate the coarser **particles.**

Mr. Ross usually adds a little crocus to the putty powder by way of coloring matter, as it is then easier to learn the quantity of powder that remains on the polishing tool, and it may be added that this is the polishing powder employed by Mr. Ross in making his improved achromatic object-glasses for astronomical telescopes.

Vienna Lime.—Vienna lime and alcohol give a beautiful polish to iron or steel. Select the soft pieces of lime, such as will be easily crushed by the thumb and finger, as they are the most free from gritty particles. Apply with a cork, piece of soft pine wood, leather, chamois, etc.

Resins.

The resins are so frequently employed in the arts that a knowledge of the action of different solvents upon them is of great value.

Dr. Sac, of Neuenberg, Switzerland, has made an extensive inquiry into the nature of different resins. The following results, as obtained by him, are given in Dingler's *Polytechnic Journal* :—The resins spoken of are copal, amber, dammar, common resins, shellac, elemi, sandarach and mastic. All these resins can be reduced to powder.

The following will become pasty before melting : Amber, shellac, elemi, sandarach and mastic ; the others will become liquid at once.

In boiling water common resin will form a semi-fluid mass ; dammar, shellac, elemi and mastic will become sticky ; while copal, amber and sandarach will remain unchanged.

Dammar and amber do not dissolve in alcohol ; copal becomes pasty ; elemi dissolves with difficulty, while resin, shellac, sandarach and mastic dissolve easily.

Acetic acid makes common resin swell ; on all the others it has no effect.

Caustic soda dissolves shellac readily ; resin partly ; but has no influence on the others.

Amber and shellac do not dissolve in sulphide of carbon ; copal becomes soft and expands ; elemi, sandarach and mastic dissolve slowly ; while resin and dammar dissolve easily.

Oil of turpentine dissolves neither amber nor shellac, but swells copal ; dissolves dammar, resin, elemi and sandarach easily, and mastic very easily.

Benzol does not dissolve copal, amber and shellac, but

does elemi and sandarach to a limited extent; while dammar, resin and mastic offer no difficulty.

Petroleum ether has no effect on copal, amber and shellac; it is a poor solvent for resin, elemi and sandarach, and a good one for dammar and mastic.

Concentrated sulphuric acid dissolves all resins, imparting to them a dark brown color, excepting dammar, which takes a brilliant red tint.

Boiling linseed oil has no effect on copal and amber; shellac, elemi and sandarach dissolve easily.

Nitric acid imparts to elemi a dirty yellow color; to mastic and sandarach a light brown; it does not affect the others.

Ammonia is indifferent to amber, dammar, shellac (?) and elemi; copal, sandarach and mastic become soft, and finally dissolve; while resin will dissolve at once.

Saws.

The grand secret of putting any saw in the best possible cutting order, consists in filing the teeth at a given angle to cut rapidly, and of a uniform length, so that the points will all touch a straight-edged rule without showing a variation of a hundredth part of an inch. Besides this, there should be just enough set in the teeth to cut a kerf as narow as it can be made, and at the same time allow the blade to work freely without pinching. On the contrary, the kerf must not be so wide as to permit the blade to rattle when in motion. The very points of the teeth do the cutting. If one tooth is a twentieth of an inch longer than two or three on each side of it, the long tooth will be required to do so much more cutting than it should, that the sawing cannot be done well. Hence the saw goes jumping along, working hard and cutting slowly. If one tooth is longer than those on either side of it, the short ones do not cut, although the points may be sharp. When putting a cross-cut saw in order, it will pay well to dress the points with an old file, and afterwards sharpen them with a fine whetstone. Much mechanical skill is requisite to put a saw in prime order. One careless thrust with a file will shorten the point of a tooth so much that it will be utterly useless, so far as cutting is concerned. The teeth should be set with much care, and the filing should be done with great accuracy. If the teeth are uneven at the points a large flat file should be secured to a block of wood in such a manner that the very points only may be jointed, so that the cutting edge of the same may be in a complete line or circle. Every tooth should cut a little as the saw is worked. The teeth of a handsaw, for all sorts of work, should be filed fleaming, or at an angle on the front edge; while the back edges may be filed fleaming, or square across the blade. The best way to file a circular saw for cutting wood across the grain, is to dress every fifth tooth square across and about one-twentieth of an inch shorter than the others, which shou'd be filed fleaming at an angle of about forty degrees.

Sieves.

It is often desirable to sift powders into different degrees of fineness, and very fine sieves are not always to be easily had. Those made of hair and wire answer well, but the finest may be made out of the bolting cloth used by millers. It may be sewed over a hoop of tin or brass, or even a ring made of iron wire, or a piece of flexible wood bent into form may answer to hold the cloth.

Shellac.

Shellac or lac is a resinous substance which, in India, flows from certain trees in the form of lucid tears, in consequence of punctures made upon their branches by a small insect.

It is found in commerce in three forms—*stick lac, seed lac* and *shellac*. Stick lac is the substance in its natural state investing the small twigs of the trees, which are generally broken off in collecting it. When separated from the twigs and partially cleansed it is known as *seed lac*. Shellac is the seed lac after it has been melted, purified and formed into thin cakes.

Shellac is very apt to be adulterated with common resin, and hence, unless when a pale lacquer is required, most artisans prefer seed lac. When lac is mixed with a little resin and colored with vermillion or ivory black it forms sealing wax.

Shellac is soluble in alcohol but not in turpentine. It is also soluble in alkaline solutions, including ammonia. A solution of borax in water dissolves it readily, and the resulting solution has been used as a cement, as a varnish, and as a basis for indelible ink. It is much used by hatters as an insoluble cement.

Clarifying Shellac Solutions.—Much trouble is generally experienced in obtaining clear solutions of shellac. If a mixture of 1 part shellac with 7 parts of alcohol of 90 per cent. is heated to a suitable temperature, it quickly clears, but as quickly becomes turbid again on cooling. The only practical method of freeing the solution from what some writers call "wax," and others "fatty acid," which is present in shellac in the proportion of 1 to 5 per cent., and is the cause of the turbidity, has hitherto been the tedious process of repeated filtration. M. Peltz recommends the following method: Shellac 1 part is dissolved in alcohol 8 parts, and allowed to stand for a few hours. Powdered chalk is then added in quantity equal to half the weight of shellac in the solution, and the latter is heated to 60° R. The greater portion of the solution clears rapidly, and the remainder may be clarified by once filtering. Carbonate of magnesia and sulphate of baryta were tried in the same way, but were not found equally efficacious.

Bleached Shellac.—When bleached by the ordinary process, shellac affords a polish for light woods, etc., that is brittle and liable to peel off, while the presence of a trace of chlorine causes metallic inlaying to become dim. These defects may be avoided by a different mode of bleaching, namely, by adding fine granulated bone-black to the solution of shellac in 90 per cent. alcohol, until a thin, pasty mass is formed, and exposing this for several days to direct sunlight, occasionally shaking it thoroughly and filtering when sufficiently bleached.

Silver.

Pure silver is quite soft, and is, therefore, generally alloyed with copper to harden it.

Silversmiths' work, after having been filed is generally rubbed, firstly, with a lump of pumice-stone and water; secondly, with a slip of water-of-Ayr stone and water; thirdly, a revolving brush with rottenstone and oil; fourthly, an old black worsted stocking with oil and rottenstone, and fifthly, it is finished with the hand alone, the deep black lustre being given with rouge of great fineness. The corners and edges are often burnished with a steel burnisher, which is lubricated with soap and water if at all.

In this case and in all others of polishing with the naked hand, it is generally found that women succeed better than men, and that some few, from the peculiar texture and condition of the skin, greatly excel in the art of polishing. The skin should be soft and very slightly moist, as the polishing powder then attaches itself conveniently, and there is just sufficient adhesion between the hand and work to make the operation proceed rapidly. A dry hand becomes hard and horny, and is liable to scratch the work, and excess of moisture is also objectionable, as the hand is then too slippery.

The plated reflectors for light-houses are cleaned with rouge, which is dusted on from a muslin bag, and rubbed over them with a clean dry wash-leather.

A thin film of oxide will nevertheless occasionally form on the surface of the reflector, and this is removed with a piece of leather, with rouge moistened with spirits of wine, which dissolves the oxide, after which the dry rubber is applied as above.

Oxidized Silver.—This is not an oxidization, but a combination with sulphur or chlorine. Sulphur, soluble sulphides, and hydrosulphuric acid blacken silver, and insoluble silver salts, and particularly the chloride of silver, rapidly blackens by solar light. Add four or five thousandths of hydrosulphate of ammonia, or of quintisulphide of potassium, to ordinary water at a temperature of $160°$ to $180°$ Fahr. When the articles are dipped into this solution an iridescent coating of silver sulphide covers them, which, after a few seconds more in the liquid, turns blue-black. Remove, rinse, scratch-brush, and burnish when desired. Use the solution when freshly prepared, or the prolonged heat will precipitate too much sulphur, and the deposit will be wanting in adherence; besides, the oxidization obtained in freshly-prepared liquors is always brighter and blacker than that produced in old solutions, which is dull and grey. If the coat of silver is too thin, and the liquor too strong, the alkaline sulphide dissolves the silver, and the underlying metal appears. In this case cleanse and silver again, and use a weaker blackening solution. Oxidized parts and gilding may be put upon the same article by the following method: After the whole surface has been gilt certain portions are covered with the resist varnish;

silver the remainder. Should the process of silvering by paste and cold rubbing be employed, the gilding should be very pale, because it is not preserved, and is deeply reddened by the sulphur liquor. When this inconvenience occurs from a too concentrated liquor, it is partly remedied by rapidly washing the article in a tepid solution of cyanide of potassium.

A very beautiful effect is produced upon the surface of silver articles, technically termed oxidizing, which gives the surface an appearance of polished steel. This can be easily effected by taking a little chloride of platinum, heating the solution and applying it to the silver where an oxidized surface is required, and allowing the solution to dry upon the silver. The darkness of the color produced varies according to the strength of the platinum solution from a light steel gray to nearly black. The effect of this process, when combined with what is termed dead work, is very pretty, and may be easily applied to medals, and similar objects.

The high appreciation in which ornaments in oxidized silver are now held, renders a notice of the following processes interesting. There are two distinct shades in use—one produced by a chloride and which has a brownish tint, and the other produced by sulphur, which has a bluish-black tint. To produce the former it is necessary to wash the article with a solution of sal ammoniac; a much more beautiful tint may, however, be obtained by employing a solution composed of equal parts of sulphate of copper and sal ammoniac in vinegar. The fine black tint may be produced by a slightly warm solution of sulphuret of potassium or sodium.

The chloride of platinum mentioned above is easily prepared as follows: Take 1 part nitric acid and 2 parts hydrochloric (muriatic) acid; mix together and add a little platinum; keep the whole at or near a boiling heat; the metal is soon dissolved, forming the solution required.

Old Silvering.—To imitate old artistic productions made of solid silver, the groundwork and hollow portions not subject to friction are covered with a blackish-red, earthy coat, the parts in relief remain with a bright lead lustre. Mix a thin paste of finely powdered plumbago with essence of turpentine, to which a small portion of red ochre may be added to imitate the copper tinge of certain old silverware;

smear this all over the articles. After drying, gently rub with a soft brush, and the reliefs are set off by cleaning with a rag dipped in spirits of wine.

To give the old silver tinge to small articles, such as buttons and rings, throw them into the above paste, rub in a bag with a large quantity of dry boxwood sawdust until the desired shade is obtained.

Cleaning Silver.—Silver being a comparatively soft metal, should never be rubbed with polishing powders capable of cutting or grinding, as the delicate surface, especially if engraved or ornamented, will be sure to have the delicate lines and work injured. In cleaning silver there are but two things that ever require to be removed—dirt and the sulphuret of silver. The latter appears as a coating on all silver articles exposed to the air, and especially on silver spoons etc., which have come in contact with sulphur or the yolk of eggs. Sulphuret or sulphide of silver is soluble in several salts, especially cyanide of potassium, hyposulphite of soda, and several salts of ammonia. Therefore, to clean silver which has been blackened with sulphur, the best plan is to dissolve off the sulphide by means of some of the chemicals named.

For the ordinary purposes of cleansing silver the best material is a thin paste of alcohol, 2 parts; ammonia, 1 part; and whiting enough to make a liquid like cream. This should be smeared or painted over the silver and allowed to stand until dry. If then brushed off with a very fine brush the silver will appear clear and bright. The alcohol and ammonia dissolve all dirt and sulphide, which are then absorbed by the whiting and removed with it.

Where really good whiting, that is to say, an article that is soft or free from grit, cannot be procured, starch may be used.

Ink Stains, To Remove from Silver—The tops and other portions of silver inkstands frequently become deeply discolored with ink, which is difficult to remove by ordinary means. It may, however, be completely eradicated by making a little chloride of lime into a paste with water, and rubbing it upon the stains.

To Dissolve the Silver off old Plated Goods.—Mix 1 oz. of finely powdered saltpetre with 10 oz. sulphuric acid, and steep the goods in this mixture. If diluted with water it acts on copper and other metals, but if very strong it dissolves the silver only, and may be used to dissolve silver off plated goods without affecting the other metals.

Silvering.

Leather, cloth, wood and similar materials are silvered by processes similar to those used for gilding, silver leaf being substituted for gold leaf. Metals may be silvered either by brazing a thin sheet of silver to the surface, or by electro-plating. Frequently, however, it is desired to lightly silver a metal surface, such as brass or copper, so as to make any figures engraved thereon appear more distinct. Clock faces, dials and the scales of thermometers and barometers are cases in point, and if the surface be well lacquered with white lacquer after being silvered, such a coating is very durable. Silvering fluids or powders containing mercury should never be used unless the articles are to be afterwards exposed to a red heat so as to drive off the mercury. A silvering fluid which is very commonly sold to housekeepers under the name of *Novargent* or *Plate Renovator*, consists merely of nitrate of mercury or quicksilver. When rubbed on a copper cent or a brass stair-rod it gives it at once a bright silvery surface, but the brightness soon fades and the article, if brass, becomes black and dirty, while if it should be a piece of plated ware it will be ruined. Stair-rods and similar articles, if well silvered with powder No. 1, and then lacquered with good lacquer, will present a white silvery appearance for a long time. Plated goods should be re-coated by the electro-plating process.

Silvering Powder.—1. Nitrate of silver, 30 grains; common salt, 30 grains; cream tartar, 200 grains. Mix. Moisten with water and rub on the article with wash leather. Gives a white silvery appearance to brass, copper, etc.

2. *Novargent.*—Add common salt to a solution of nitrate of silver until the silver has all been precipitated. Wash the white precipitate or chloride of silver and add a strong solution of hyposulphite of soda until the white chloride is dissolved. Mix the resulting clear liquid with pipe-clay which has been finely powdered and thoroughly washed.

3. 1 oz. of nitrate of silver dissolved in 1 quart of rain or distilled water. When thoroughly dissolved, add a few crystals of hyposulphite of soda, which will at first form a brown precipitate, but which redissolves if sufficient hypo-

sulphite has been employed. The solution may be used by simply dipping a sponge in it, and rubbing it over the article to be coated. A solution of gold may be made and used in the same manner.

4. *Silvering Amalgam.*—A coating of silver, heavier than can be obtained by the above, may be given by the following process: Precipitate silver from its solution in nitric acid by means of copper. Take of this powder ½ oz.; common salt, 2 oz.; sal ammoniac, 2 oz.; and corrosive sublimate, 1 drachm. Make into a paste with water. Having carefully cleaned the copper surface that is to be plated, boil it in a solution of tartar and alum, rub it with the above paste, heat red hot and then polish.

Size.

The size used for filling the pores of plaster, wood, cloth, paper, etc., for the purpose of preparing it to receive paint or varnish, is usually made from glue. Where large quantities are used the size is obtained in barrels from the glue factory, and as the trouble and expense of concentrating it into cakes is thus avoided, it may be obtained at a very cheap rate. Size may be made by any one from clippings of skins, tendons, etc., boiled down to jelly and carefully freed from fat. Very fine size is prepared from parchment clippings. Where size is made from glue the following directions will prove useful:

Sizing for Window Shades.—Stretch the muslin well upon the frame. Soak over night one-half pound of the best white glue in 4 gallons water; in the morning turn it off and boil the glue. It must be very thin. Add a small piece of castile soap scraped fine. To have it more transparent add 2 oz. powdered alum. It must be put on quick, while warm. Gamboge for painting shades must be dissolved in alcohol; carmine in spirits of hartshorn.

Size for Improving Poor Drawing Paper.—Take 1 oz. of white glue, 1 oz. of white soap, and ½ oz. of alum. Soak the glue and the soap in water until they appear like jelly; then simmer in 1 quart of water until the whole is melted. Add the alum, simmer again and filter. To be applied hot.

Gold Size.—This is an entirely different article, and is in reality a very strong drying oil colored to resemble gold, and used for cementing gold leaf to articles that are to be gilt.

To prepare it, drying or boiled oil is thickened with yellow ochre or calcined red ochre, and carefully reduced to the utmost smoothness by grinding. It is thinned with oil of turpentine. It improves by age.

Skins—Tanning and Curing.

Curing Fur Skins.—The following are the directions given in the "Trapper's Guide," by Newhouse, an experienced trapper and hunter. 1. As soon as possible after the animal is dead, attend to the skinning and curing. The slightest taint of putrefaction loosens the fur and destroys the value of the skin. 2. Scrape off all superfluous flesh and fat, but be careful not to go so deep as to cut the fibre of the skin. 3. Never dry a skin by the fire or in the sun, but in a cool, shady place, sheltered from rain. If you use a barn door for a stretcher, nail the skin on the *inside* of the door. 4. Never use "preparations" of any kind in curing skins, nor even wash them in water, but simply stretch and dry them as they are taken from the animal. In drying skins it is important that they should be stretched tight like a drum-head.

To prepare Sheep Skins for Mats.—1. Make a strong soap lather with hot water and let it stand till cold; wash the fresh skin in it, carefully squeezing out all the dirt from the wool; wash it in cold water till all the soap is taken out. Dissolve a pound each of salt and alum in 2 gallons of hot water, and put the skin into a tub sufficient to cover it; let it soak for 12 hours and hang it over a pole to drain. When well drained, stretch it carefully on a board to dry, and stretch several times while drying. Before it is quite dry sprinkle on the flesh side 1 oz. each of finely pulverized alum and saltpetre, rubbing them in well. Try if the wool be firm on the skin; if not, let it remain a day or two, then rub again with alum; fold the flesh sides together and hang in the shade for two or three days, turning them over each day till quite dry. Scrape the flesh side with a blunt knife and rub it with pumice or rotten stone. Very beautiful mittens can be made of lambs' skins prepared in this way.

2. The following process has been found to succeed very well with sheep skins, dog skins and similar hides: Tack the skin upon a board with the flesh side out, and then scrape with a blunt knife; next rub it over hard with pulverized chalk, until it will absorb no more. Then take the skin off

from the board and cover it with pulverized alum; double half-way over, with the flesh side in contact; then roll tight together and keep dry for three days, after which unfold and stretch it again on a board or floor, and dry in the air, and it will be ready for use.

Skins of Rabbits, Cats and small Animals.—Lay the skin on a smooth board, the fur side undermost, and fasten it down with tinned tacks. Wash it over first with a solution of salt; then dissolve 2½ oz. of alum in 1 pint of warm water, and with a sponge dipped in this solution, moisten the surface all over; repeat this every now and then for three days. When the skin is quite dry take out the tacks, and rolling it loosely the long way, the hair side in, draw it quickly backwards and forwards through a large smooth ring until it is quite soft, and then roll it in the contrary way of the skin and repeat the operation. Skins prepared in this way are useful in many experiments, and they make good gloves and chest protectors.

Stains.

Stains of different kinds are removed either by dissolving the offensive matter out of the material which it has soiled or by destroying it. Ordinary washing is a good example of the first method; the removal of fruit stains by means of chloride of lime illustrates the second. Sometimes it is necessary to combine both methods. In practice it is of course necessary to avoid the use of any solvent or bleaching agent that can injure the material from which the stain is to be removed. The following is a list of the stains which most frequently occur, and also of the best methods of removing them:

Acids.—Most acids produce red stains in all black or blue colors of vegetable origin. Where the acid has not been so strong as to injure the texture of the fabric, such stains may be easily removed by the use of a little potash, soda or ammonia. Nitric acid, however, not only turns red, but bleaches the goods, and it is very difficult to remove stains caused by this acid. It is said that the yellow stains formed on brown or black woolen goods by nitric acid can be removed, when freshly formed, by moistening them repeatedly with a concentrated solution of permanganate of potash, and then rinsing with water. Yellow stains on the hands may be treated in the same way, and the dark brown coloration produced may then be removed by treating with aqueous solution of sulphurous acid.

Aniline Dyes.—A solution of common sodium sulphite will rapidly remove the stains of most of the aniline dyes from the hands.

Fruit Stains.—Most fruits yield juices which, owing to the acid they contain, permanently injure the tone of the dye; but the greater part may be removed without leaving a stain, if the spot be rinsed in cold water in which a few drops of aqua ammoniæ have been placed, before the spot has dried. Wine stains on white materials may be removed by rinsing with cold water, applying locally a weak solution of chloride of lime, and again rinsing in an abundance of water. Some fruit stains yield only to soaping with the hand, followed by fumigation with sulphurous acid; but the latter process is inadmissible with certain colored stuffs. If delicate colors are injured by soapy or alkaline matters, the stains must be treated with colorless vinegar of moderate strength.

Grease.—1. Where the fabric will bear it, the best method of removing grease spots is simple washing with soap and water. No ordinary grease spot will resist this.

2. Chalk, fuller's-earth, steatite or "French chalk." These should be merely diffused through a little water to form a thin paste, which is spread upon the spot, allowed to dry, and then brushed out.

3. Ox-gall and yolk of egg, which have the property of dissolving fatty bodies without affecting perceptibly the texture or colors of cloth. The oxgall should be purified, to prevent its greenish tint from degrading the brilliancy of dyed stuffs, or the purity of whites. Thus prepared it is the most effective of all substances known for removing this kind of stains, especially for woolen cloths. It is to be diffused through its own bulk of water, applied to the spots, rubbed well into them with the hands till they disappear, after which the stuff is to be washed with soft water.

4. The volatile oil of turpentine. This will take out only recent stains; for which purpose it ought to be previously purified by distillation over quicklime.

5. Benzine or essence of petroleum is commonly used for removing grease spots; but these liquids present the inconvenience of leaving, in most cases, a brownish *aureola*. To

avoid this, it is necessary, whilst the fabric is still saturated, and immediately the stain has disappeared, to sprinkle gypsum or lycopodium over the whole of the moistened surface. When dry, the powder is brushed away.

5. Balls for removing grease spots are made as follows: Take fuller's-earth, free from all gritty matter; mix with half a pound of the earth, so prepared, half a pound of soda, as much soap, and eight yolks of eggs well beaten up with half a pound of purified ox-gall. The whole must be triturated upon a porphyry slab; the soda with the soap in the same manner as colors are ground, mixing in gradually the eggs and the ox-gall previously beaten together. Incorporate next the soft earth by slow degrees, till a uniform thick paste be formed, which should be made into balls or cakes of a convenient size, and laid out to dry. A little of this detergent being scraped off with a knife, made into a paste with water, and applied to the stain, will remove it.

Ink and Iron Mould.—Fresh ink and the soluble salts of iron produce stains which, if allowed to dry, and especially if afterwards the material has been washed, are difficult to extract without injury to the ground. When fresh, such stains yield rapidly to a treatment with moistened cream of tartar, aided by a little friction, if the material or color is delicate. If the ground be white, oxalic acid, employed in the form of a concentrated aqueous solution, will effectually remove fresh iron stains.

A concentrated solution of pyrophosphate of soda removes many kinds of ink from delicate fabrics without altering the coloring matters printed upon the tissues, or in any way injuring them.

Mildew.—Make a very weak solution of chloride of lime in water (about a heaped-up teaspoonful to a quart of water); strain it carefully, and dip the spot on the garment into it; and if the mildew does not disappear immediately, lay it in the sun for a few minutes, or dip it again into the solution. The work is effectually and speedily done, and the chloride of lime neither rots the cloth nor removes delicate colors, when sufficiently diluted, and the articles well rinsed afterward in clear water.

Another method is to wet the spot in lemon juice, then spread over it soft soap and chalk mixed together, and spread where the hottest rays of the sun will beat upon it for half an hour; if not entirely removed repeat the same. Or wet in clear lemon juice and lay in the sun; or soak for an hour or two, and then spread in the sun.

Nitrate of Silver.—Nitrate of silver, it will be remembered, is the base of most of the so-called indelible inks used for marking linen in almost every household. Stains or marks of any kind made with silver solution or the bath solution of photographers may be promptly removed from clothing by simply wetting the stain or mark with a solution of bichloride of mercury. The chemical result is the change of the black-looking nitrate of silver into chloride of silver, which is white or invisible on the cloth. Bichloride of mercury can be had at the drug stores. It is slightly soluble in water, is a rank poison, and we would not advise anybody to keep it about one's house.

The immediate and repeated application of a very weak solution of cyanide of potassium (accompanied by thorough rinsings in clean water), will generally remove these stains without injury to the colors.

Paint.—Stains of oil-paint may be removed with bisulphide of carbon; many by means of spirits of turpentine; if dry and old, with chloroform. For these last, as well as for tar-spots, the best way is to cover them with olive oil or butter. When the paint is softened, the whole may be removed by treatment, first, with spirits of turpentine, then with benzine.

Tar.—Tar and pitch produce stains easily removed by successive applications of spirits of turpentine, coal-tar naphtha, and benzine. If they are very old and hard, it is well to soften them by lightly rubbing with a pledget of wool dipped in good olive oil. The softened mass will then easily yield to the action of the other solvents. Resins, varnishes and sealing wax may be removed by warming and applying strong alcohol. Care must always be taken that, in rubbing the material to remove the stains, the friction shall be applied the way of the stuff, and not indifferently backwards and forwards.

Steel—Working and Tempering.

Most workmen find themselves, at times, compelled to forge and temper their own tools, such as drills, cold chisels, etc. The following hints will be of service:

Forging Steel.—Beware of over-heating the piece to be

forged, and also be careful that the fire is free from sulphur. Small drills are easily heated in the flame of a lamp or candle; a Bunsen burner will heat sufficiently quite a good sized tool. Charcoal makes the best fire for all kinds of tools. If you are compelled to use common bituminous coal let the fire burn until most of the sulphur has been driven off. Do not hammer with heavy blows after the steel has cooled. By tapping it lightly, however, until it becomes black, the closeness of the grain is increased.

To Restore burnt Cast Steel.—Heat it to a bright cherry red and quench it in water. Do this a few times and then forge it carefully, and it will be nearly as good as before. The various recipes for mixtures for restoring burnt steel are worthless.

Hardening and Tempering Steel.—Heat the steel to a bright cherry red and plunge it in water that has been thoroughly boiled and then allowed to cool. It will then be "as hard as fire and water will make it," and too hard for anything except hardened bearings, or tools for cutting and drilling glass and very hard metals.

Where very hard tools are required, as, for example, for cutting steel or glass, mercury is the best liquid for hardening steel tools. The best steel, when forged into shape and hardened in mercury, will cut almost anything. We have seen articles made from ordinary steel, which have been hardened and tempered to a deep straw color, turned with comparative ease with cutting tools, from good tool steel hardened in mercury.

To make it stand work without breaking, it must be *tempered*. To do this, polish the surface on a grindstone or with emery paper, so that any change in the color of the metal may be easily seen. Then heat the tool until the cutting edge shows the proper color, as given below. Large drills and cold chisels are hardened and tempered at one operation, the cutting edge being cooled and hardened while the upper part is left hot. When taken from the water the heat from the shank passes towards the cutting edge and brings it to the right degree of softness. Small drills may be best tempered in the flame of a lamp. A spirit lamp is best, and the neatest plan is to heat the drill a short distance from the point and allow the heat to flow towards the cutting edge. As soon as the right color is seen on the edge, the entire tool is plunged in water and cooled. In this way the shank is kept soft and the tool is not so apt to snap off.

The following are the degrees of heat (Fahrenheit) and corresponding colors to which tools for different purposes should be brought:

Temperature.	Color.	Temper.
430°	Very faint yellow.	Very hard; suitable for hammer faces, drills for stone, etc.
450°	Pale straw color.	
470°	Full yellow.	Hard and inelastic; suitable for shears, scissors, turning tools for hard metal, etc.
490°	Brown.	
510°	Brown with purple spots.	Suitable for tools for cutting wood and soft metals, such as plane irons, knives, etc.
538°	Purple.	
550°	Dark blue.	For tools requiring strong cutting edges without extreme hardness; as cold chisels, axes, cutlery, etc.
560°	Full blue.	
600°	Grayish blue verging on black.	Spring temper; saws, swords.

To Temper Steel on one Edge.—Red hot lead is an excellent thing in which to heat a long plate of steel that requires softening or tempering on one edge. The steel need only to be heated at the part required, and there is little danger of the metal warping or springing. By giving sufficient time, thick portions may be heated equally with thin parts. The ends of wire springs that are to be bent or riveted may be softened for that purpose by this process, after the springs have been hardened or tempered.

Blazing Off.—Saws and springs are generally hardened in various compositions of oil, suet, wax and other ingredients, which, however, lose their hardening property after a few weeks constant use; the saws are heated in long furnaces, and then immersed horizontally and edgewise in a long trough containing the composition; two troughs are commonly used, the one until it gets too warm, then the other for a period, and so on alternately. Part of the composition is wiped off the saws with a piece of leather, when they are removed from the trough, and they are heated, one by one, over a clear coke fire, until the grease inflames; this is called "blazing off."

The composition used by an experienced saw maker is two pounds of suet and a quarter of a pound of beeswax to every gallon of whale oil; these are boiled together, and will serve for thin works and most kinds of steel. The addition of black resin, to the extent of about one pound to the gallon, makes it serve for thicker pieces, and for those it refused to harden before; but the resin should be added with judgment, or the works will become too hard and brittle. The composition is useless when it has been constantly employed for about a month; the period depends, however, on the extent to which it is used, and the trough should be thoroughly cleansed out before new mixture is placed in it.

The following recipe is recommended: Twenty gallons of spermaceti oil; twenty pounds of beef suet, rendered; one gallon of neatsfoot oil; one pound of pitch; three pounds of black resin.

These last two articles must be previously melted together, and then added to the other ingredients; when the whole must be heated in a proper iron vessel, with a close cover fitted to it, until the moisture is entirely evaporated, and the composition will take fire on a flaming body being presented to its surface, but which must be instantly extinguished again by putting on the cover of the vessel.

When the saws are wanted to be rather hard, but little of the grease is burned off; when milder, a larger portion; and for a spring temper, the whole is allowed to burn away.

When the work is thick, or irregularly thick and thin, as in some springs, a second and third dose is burned off, to insure equality of temper at all parts alike.

Gun-lock springs are sometimes literally fried in oil for a considerable time over a fire in an iron tray; the thick parts are then sure to be sufficiently reduced, and the thin parts do not become the more softened from the continuance of the blazing heat. But for ordinary steel articles which are required to be soft, tough and springy, the usual plan is to harden and then dip them in any coarse oil, and heat them over the fire until the oil blazes.

Springs and saws appear to lose their elasticity, after hardening and tempering, from the reduction and friction they undergo in grinding and polishing. Toward the conclusion of the manufacture, the elasticity of the saw is restored, principally by hammering, and partly by heating it over a clear coke fire to a straw color; the tint is removed by very diluted muriatic acid, after which the saws are well washed in plain water and dried.

Welding Steel.—As we have already stated in the article on *Iron*, welding is in reality a species of autogenous soldering. And, as in soldering or brazing, it is necessary to keep the surfaces that are to be united, free from dirt and oxide, so in welding, the surfaces must be perfectly clean or the joint will be imperfect. In welding common iron, sand is the flux generally used. When it is required to weld steel to iron, the steel must be heated to a less degree than the iron, as it is the most fusible. The surfaces should be thoroughly cleaned before they are brought together. Sal ammoniac cleans the dirt from the steel, and borax causes the oxide to fuse before it attains that heat which will burn the steel; consequently, a mixture of these two substances forms one of the best materials for welding.

The best mode of preparing this mixture is as follows: Take ten parts of borax and one part of sal ammoniac and grind them together. Then melt them together, and when cold reduce the mixture to fine powder, and preserve in a well-stopped jar or bottle.

To Blue Steel.—The mode employed in bluing steel is merely to subject it to heat. The dark blue is produced at a temperature of 600°, the full blue at 500°, and the blue at 550°. The steel must be finely polished on its surface, and then exposed to a uniform degree of heat. Accordingly, there are three ways of coloring; first, by a flame producing no soot, as spirits of wine; secondly, by a hot plate of iron; and thirdly, by wood ashes. As a very regular degree of heat is necessary, wood ashes for fine work are to be preferred. The work must be covered over with them, and carefully watched; when the color is sufficiently heightened, the work is perfect.

To Blue Small Steel Articles.—Make a box of sheet iron; fill it with sand and subject it to a steady heat. The articles to be blued must be finished and well polished. Immerse the articles in the sand, keeping watch of them until they are of the right color, when they should be taken out and immersed in oil.

Sulphur.

Sulphur or brimstone is a well-known yellow substance largely used in the manufacture of matches, gunpowder and sulphuric acid. Aside from these uses, which are of interest only to large manufacturers, sulphur is employed for bleaching, disinfecting, making moulds for plaster casts, and as a cement for fastening iron bars in stone sockets.

Sulphur, when burned, produces sulphurous acid, a gas which destroys most vegetable colors and the germs of most diseases. As a bleaching agent it is sometimes to be preferred to chlorine, as it does not injure the fabrics so much. The method of using it is to hang the articles to be bleached in a large box or closet in which the sulphur is afterwards burned. The easiest way to burn the sulphur is to dip heavy brown paper in melted sulphur, and burn the matches thus produced. In this way the sulphur is exposed to the air sufficiently to cause it to continue to burn when once ignited. Another very good plan is to place the sulphur on a block of iron or brick which has been previously heated to above the melting point of sulphur. The sulphur, if then ignited, will continue to burn freely, but it is almost impossible to get a cold mass of sulphur to burn freely.

The same method answers for disinfecting rooms, and sulphurous acid vapors are the least injurious and most easily procured of all our disinfectants. The National Board of Health, in their recent "Instructions for Disinfection," say that "fumigation with sulphur is the only practicable method for disinfecting the house. For this purpose the rooms to be disinfected must be vacated. Heavy clothing, blankets, bedding, etc., should be opened and exposed during the fumigation. Close the rooms as tightly as possible, ignite the sulphur, and allow the room to remain closed for twenty-four hours. For a room about ten feet square at least two pounds of sulphur should be used; for larger rooms, proportionally increased quantities." Of course in making arrangements for burning the sulphur great care must be exercised so as not to set the floor on fire. Safety is best secured by placing the burning sulphur over a tub of water or a considerable heap of sand or soil.

In making moulds for taking plaster casts, the sulphur must be rendered plastic. This is an extraordinary property possessed by this material, and one known only to chemists and experts. When sulphur is melted and poured into water, instead of becoming hard it remains quite soft like dough, and in this state it may be pressed into the most minute crevices of a medal or other object, so as to take a perfect mould of it. From this mould plaster casts or electrotypes may be taken. After a short time the sulphur returns to its original hard, yellow, brittle condition.

As a cement for fastening iron rods in the holes sunk in stones, as in the gratings of windows and the iron work of fences, sulphur is now extensively used instead of lead. To pure sulphur, however, there is this very strong objection that it is exceedingly brittle and is readily fractured, and even reduced to coarse powder by sudden changes of temperature. We have seen a huge roll of sulphur broken simply by the heat of the hand. This may be avoided, in a measure, by mixing the melted sulphur with some inert powder like sand. Iron filings have also been mixed with it for the purpose.

Tin.

Tin is a brilliant, silvery-white metal. It is very malleable, but its power to resist tensile strains is so small that it is not very ductile. When bent it emits a peculiar crackling sound, arising from the destruction of cohesion amongst its particles. When a bar of tin is rapidly bent backwards and forwards several times successively, it becomes so hot that it cannot be held in the hand.

Tin is acted upon by caustic alkalies (potash and soda), but resists the acids of fruit, etc.; hence its use for coating iron so as to prevent corrosion and rust. Tin plate is sheet iron which has been coated with tin. To apply the tin the iron must be heated, and this is apt, in some cases, to injure the articles to be tinned, as it softens the iron, or in other words draws its temper. The process described under the head "Iron," page 70, enables us to avoid this difficulty.

Tin forms alloys with various metals, those of lead and copper being best known. That with lead is known as solder and pewter (see under these heads); that with copper is bronze, gun metal or "composition."

Tin and iron may be fused together in all proportions, forming apparently homogeneous alloys. Berthier describes one containing 35·1 per cent. of tin, and another containing 50 per cent. of tin, both being very brittle and capable of being reduced to an impalpable powder. The affinity of iron for tin is also well illustrated in common tin plate, which is nothing more than sheet iron superficially combined with tin, to which a further quantity adheres without being in combination. The alloy of tin and iron upon the plate, however, is so thin that it can easily be removed by mechanical friction, and the amount of tin thus alloyed is probably not much larger than one-half of one per cent. Tin, when added to pig iron, imparts to it a steel-like texture of fine grain and great hardness without very great brittleness. Such iron is easily fused, and gives a sound like a bell. Indeed, in the Great International Exhibition of 1851, there was a large bell of cast iron stated to be alloyed with a small proportion of tin. According to Karsten, pig iron with one per cent. of tin yields a somewhat cold-short wrought iron with about 0·19 per cent. of tin. Such iron, it is stated, works well under the hammer, but at a white heat white vapors escape. With more tin, the iron in welding gave much waste and produced cold-short iron, with a fine, white and dull grain. For specific purposes, however, especially where great hardness is required, iron with a small amount of tin, not exceeding 0·3 per cent. seems to be well adapted. Sterling, in England, hardens the tops of rails with tin, and according to a report of the English Commission for testing iron in regard to its adaptability for railroad purposes, the best Dundyvan bar iron, if alloyed with 0·22 per cent. of tin, supported, without breaking, a weight of 23·39 tons to the square inch. Ott fused wrought iron with 0·5 per cent. of tin, and arrived at results similar to those of Karsten. Whilst at a welding heat it worked very well, the smith stating that it was some of the toughest iron he had ever worked. The grain was found to be fine and steel-like, with strong lustre and bright color.

Varnish.

It is in general more economical to buy varnishes than to make them on the small scale. Occasionally, however, our readers may find themselves in a situation where a simple recipe for a good varnish will prove valuable. We give a few recipes which are easily followed, and which will undoubtedly prove useful in special cases.

Basket Ware, Varnish for.—The following varnish for

basket work is said to dry rapidly, to possess sufficient elasticity, and to be applicable with or without admixture of color: Heat 375 grains of good linseed oil on a sand bath until it becomes stringy, and a drop placed on a cold, inclined surface does not run; then add gradually 7,500 grains of copal oil varnish, or any other copal varnish. As considerable effervescence takes place, a large vessel is necessary. The desired consistency is given to it, when cold, by addition of oil of turpentine.

Black Varnish for Optical Work.—The external surfaces of brass and iron are generally blacked or bronzed with compositions given under the head of *lacquers*. The insides of the tubes of telescopes and microscopes should be coated with a dead black varnish so as to absorb the light and prevent any glare. The varnish that is generally used for this purpose consists of lampblack, made liquid by means of a very thin solution of shellac in alcohol, but such varnish, even when laid on warm metal, is very apt to scale off and thus produce two serious evils—the exposure of the bright metallic surface and the deposit of specks on the lenses. It will therefore be found that lampblack, carefully ground in turpentine, to which about a fifth of its volume of gold size or boiled linseed oil has been added, will adhere much more firmly. The metal should be warm when the varnish is applied. Care must be taken not to use too much gold size, otherwise the effect will be a bright black instead of a dead black.

Black Varnish for Cast Iron.—1. For those objects to which it is applicable one of the best black varnishes is obtained by applying boiled linseed oil to the iron, the latter being heated to a temperature that will just char or blacken the oil. The oil seems to enter into the pores of the iron, and after such an application the metal resists rust and corrosive agents very perfectly.

2. Fuse 40 oz. of asphaltum and add ½ a gallon of boiled linseed oil, 6 oz. red lead, 6 oz. litharge, and 4 oz. sulphate of zinc, dried and powdered. Boil for two hours and mix in 8 oz. fused dark amber gum and a pint of hot linseed oil, and boil again for two hours more. When the mass has thickened withdraw the heat and thin down with a gallon of turpentine.

Green Varnish.—There is a most beautiful transparent

green varnish employed to give a fine glittering color to gilt or other decorated works. As the preparation of this varnish is very little known, an account of it may in all probability prove of interest to many of our readers. The process is as follows : Grind a small quantity of a peculiar pigment called "Chinese blue," along with about double the quantity of finely-powdered chromate of potash, and a sufficient quantity of copal varnish thinned with turpentine. The mixture requires the most elaborate grinding or incorporating of its ingredients, otherwise it will not be transparent, and therefore useless for the purpose for which it is intended. The "tone" of the color may be varied by an alteration in the proportion of the ingredients. A preponderance of chromate of potash causes a yellowish shade in the green, as might have been expected, and *vice versa* with the blue under the same circumstances. This colored varnish will produce a very striking effect in japanned goods, paper hangings, etc., and can be made at a very cheap rate.

Iron Work, Bright Varnish for.—Dissolve 3 lbs. of resin in 10 pints boiled linseed oil, and add 2 lbs. of turpentine.

Map Varnish.—Clear Canada balsam, 4 oz.; turpentine, 8 oz. Warm gently and shake until dissolved. Maps, drawings, etc., which are to be varnished with this solution, should be first brushed over with a solution of isinglass and allowed to dry thoroughly.

Mastic.—Mastic, 6 oz.; turpentine, 1 quart. Tough, hard, brilliant and colorless. Excellent for common woodwork.

Metals—Bright, Varnish for.—In order to make alcoholic varnish adhere more firmly to polished metallic surfaces, A. Morell adds one part of pure crystallized boracic acid to 200 parts of the varnish. Thus prepared it adheres so firmly to the metal that it cannot be scratched off with the finger nail ; it appears, in fact, like a glaze. If more boracic acid is added than above recommended the varnish loses its intensity of color.

Paintings, Varnish for.—A good varnish can be made as follows : Mastic, six ounces ; pure turpentine, one-half ounce ; camphor, two drachms ; spirits of turpentine, nineteen ounces ; add first the camphor to the turpentine. The mixture is made in a water-bath, and when the solution is effected, add the mastic and the spirits of turpentine near the end of the operation, then filter through a cotton cloth. The varnish should be laid on very carefully.

Rust, Varnish for Preventing.—A varnish for this purpose may be made of 120 parts resin, 180 sandarac, 50 gumlac. They should be heated gradually until melted, and thoroughly mixed, then 120 parts turpentine added, and subsequently, after further heating, 180 parts rectified alcohol. After careful filtration, it should be put into tightly-corked bottles.

Shellac Varnish.—Dissolve good shellac or seed lac in alcohol, making the varnish of any consistence desired. NOTE.—Shellac gives a pale cinnamon colored varnish. Varnish made with seed lac is deeper colored and redder. If colorless varnish is desired use bleached shellac, an article which is to be had at most drug stores.

Tortoise Shell Japan.—Take good linseed oil, one gallon; amber, one-half pound; boil together until the fluid is brown and thick. Then strain through a cloth and boil again until of consistency of pitch, when it is fit for use. Having prepared this varnish well, clean the article to be japanned, and then brush the parts over with vermillion mixed with shellac varnish, or with drying oil diluted with turpentine. When this coat is dry, brush the whole with the amber varnish diluted to a proper consistency with turpentine, and then, when set firm, put the article into a hot stove to undergo heat for as long a time as required to produce the desired effect. In some instances as much as two weeks may be required, after which finish in an annealing oven.

Turpentine Varnish.—Clear pale resin, 5 lbs.; turpentine, 7 lbs. Dissolve in any convenient vessel.

Varnish for Violins and similar articles.—Sandarach, 6 oz.; mastic, 3 oz.; turpentine varnish, one-half pint; alcohol 1 gallon. Keep in a tight tin can in a warm place until the gums are dissolved.

Varnish for Replacing Turpentine and Linseed Oil Paints.—Fr. Theis, of Bissendorf, prepares a varnish consisting of 100 parts of resin, 20 parts of crystallized carbonate of soda, and 50 parts of water, by heating these substances together and mixing them with a solution of 24 parts of strong liquor ammonia in 250 parts of water. With the mass thus obtained the pigments are levigated without the addition of linseed oil or turpentine; the paint dries readily without the aid of a drier and looks very well, especially when varnished. The paint keeps well, even under water, and becomes very hard,

The cost is said to be about one-third that of ordinary oil paints.

White, Hard Varnish for Wood or Metal.—Mastic, 2 oz.; sandarach, 8 oz.; elemi, 1 oz.; Strasbourg or Scio turpentine, 4 oz.; alcohol, 1 quart.

White Varnish for Paper, Wood or Linen.—Sandarach, 8 oz.; mastic, 2 oz.; Canada balsam, 4 oz.; alcohol, 1 quart.

White Spirit Varnish.—Rectified spirit, 1 gallon; gum sandarach, 2½ lbs. Put these ingredients into a tin bottle, warm gently and shake till dissolved. Then add a pint of pale turpentine varnish.

Wood, Parisian Varnish for.—To prepare a good varnish for fancy woods, dissolve one part of good shellac in three to four parts of alcohol of 92 per cent. in a water-bath, and cautiously add distilled water until a curdy mass separates out, which is collected and pressed between linen; the liquid is filtered through paper, all the alcohol removed by distillation from the water bath, and the resin removed and dried at 100° centigrade until it ceases to lose weight; it is then dissolved in double its weight of alcohol of at least 96 per cent., and the solution perfumed with lavender oil.

Wood—Stained, Varnish for.—A solution of four ounces of sandarac, one ounce gum mastic, and four ounces shellac, in one pound of alcohol, to which two ounces oil of turpentine is added, can be recommended as a varnish over stained woods.

Varnishing.

Before beginning to varnish, it is necessary that the surface to which it is to be applied, should be perfectly free from all grease and smoke stains, for it will be found if this is not attended to, the varnish will not dry hard. If the varnish is to be applied to old articles, it is necessary to wash them very carefully with soap and water before applying it. When it is wished that the varnish should dry quickly and hard, it is necessary to be careful that the varnish should always be kept as long a time as possible before being used; and also that too high a temperature has not been used in manufacturing the varnish employed. It is likewise customary, when it can be done, to expose the article to the atmosphere of a heated room. This is called stoving it, and is found to greatly improve the appearance of the work, as well as to cause the varnish to dry quickly. After the surface is varnished, to remove all the marks left by the brush, it is usually carefully polished with finely-powdered pumice stone and water. Afterwards, to give the surface the greatest polish it is capable of receiving, it is rubbed over with a clean soft rag, on the surface of which a mixture of very finely powdered tripoli and oil has been applied. The surface is afterwards cleaned with a soft rag and powdered starch, and the last polish is given with the palm of the hand. This method is, however, only employed when those varnishes are used which, when dry, become sufficiently hard to admit of it.

A good surface may be produced on unpainted wood by the following treatment: Glass-paper the wood thoroughly as for French polishing, size it, and lay on a coat of varnish, very thin, with a piece of sponge or wadding covered with a piece of linen rag. When dry, rub down with pumice dust, and apply a second coat of varnish. Three or four coats should produce a surface almost equal to French polish, if the varnish is good and the pumice dust be well applied between each coat. The use of a sponge or wadding instead of a brush aids in preventing the streaky appearance usually caused by a brush in the hands of an unskilled person.

When varnish is laid on a piece of cold furniture or a cold carriage-body, even after it has been spread evenly and with dispatch, it will sometimes "crawl" and roll this way and that way as if it were a liquid possessing vitality and the power of locomotion. It is sometimes utterly impossible to varnish an article at all satisfactorily during cold weather and in a cold apartment. In cold and damp weather a carriage, chair or any other article to be varnished should be kept in a clean and warm apartment where there is no dust flying, until the entire woodwork and iron-work have been warmed through and through, to a temperature equal to that of summer heat—say eighty degrees. That temperature should be maintained day and night. If a fire is kept for only eight or ten hours during the day, the furniture will be cold, even in a warm paint-room. Before any varnish is applied, some parts of the surface which may have been handled frequently, should be rubbed with a woolen cloth dipped in spirits of turpentine, so as to remove any greasy, oleaginous matter which may have accumulated. Table-beds, backs of chairs, and fronts of bureau drawers are sometimes so thoroughly glazed over that varnish will not adhere to the surface, any more than water will lie smoothly on recently painted casings. The varnish should also be warm—not hot—and it should be spread quickly and evenly. As soon as it flows from the brush readily and spreads evenly, and before it commences to set, let the rubbing or brushing cease. One can always do a better job by laying on a coat of medium heaviness, rather than a very light coat or a covering so heavy that the varnish will hang down in ridges. Varnish must be of the proper consistency, in order to flow just right and to set with a smooth surface. If it is either too thick or too thin one cannot do a neat job.

When it is wished to varnish drawings, engravings, or other paper articles, it is usual to give them a coat of size before applying the varnish. For the preparation of *Size* see article under that head.

To Restore Spotted Varnish.—If the varnish has been blistered by heat or corroded by strong acids, the only remedy is to scrape or sandpaper the article and revarnish. Spots may often be removed by the following process: Make a mixture of equal parts of linseed oil, alcohol and turpentine, *slightly* moisten a rag with it, and rub the spots until they disappear. Then polish the spot with ordinary blotting paper. Varnish injured by heat can hardly be restored in any other way than by removing it and applying a fresh coat.

Voltaic Batteries.

In every kind of battery it is essential that the connections be bright, and that the metal surfaces which are to be united should be brought together under considerable pressure. Those batteries which depend for contact upon light springs, and the mere placing of wires in holes, lose a great deal of available power. The surfaces ought invariably to be filed bright and pressed together by means of screws. We have frequently seen the action of the batteries used for medical purposes entirely stopped by a thin film of oxide.

The zincs also should always be thoroughly amalgamated to prevent waste. When the zincs are new and uncorroded, amalgamation is an easy process. Dip the zincs in dilute sulphuric acid (8 parts water and 1 of acid), and rub them with mercury. The mercury will adhere quite readily and render the entire surface brilliant and silvery. But when the zincs are old and corroded it will be found that the mercury does not adhere to some parts. In such cases wash the surface of the zinc with a solution of nitrate of mercury and it will become coated with amalgam. Once the surface is touched, it is easy to add as much mercury as may be desired by simply rubbing on the liquid metal.

The coating of mercury adds greatly to the durability of the zincs, as when so prepared the acid will not act on them except when the current is passing, and from the excellent condition of the entire surface the power of the battery is greatly increased.

Watch—Care of.

1. Wind your watch as nearly as possible at same hour every day. 2. Be careful that the key is in good condition, as there is much danger of injuring the works when the key is worn or cracked; there are more main springs and chains broken through a jerk in winding than from any other cause, which injury will sooner or later be the result if the key be in bad order. 3. As all metals contract by cold and expand by heat, it must be manifest that to keep the watch as nearly as possible at one temperature, is a necessary piece of attention. 4. Keep the watch as constantly as possible in one position, that is, if it hangs by day let it hang by night, against something soft. 5. The hands of a pocket chronometer or duplex watch should never be set backwards; in other watches this a matter of no consequence. 6. The glass should never be opened in watches which set and regulate at the back. One or two directions more it is of vital importance that you bear in mind. On regulating a watch, should it be fast, move the regulator a trifle towards the slow; and if going slow, do the reverse; you cannot move the regulator too slightly or too gently at a time, and the only inconvenience that can arise is having to perform the operation more than once. On the contrary, if you move the regulator too much at a time, you will be as far, if not further than ever, from attaining your object, so that you may repeat the movement until quite tired and disappointed, stoutly blaming both watch and watchmaker, while the fault is entirely your own. Again, you cannot be too careful in respect of the

nature and condition of your watch-pocket; see that it be made of something soft and pliant, such as wash-leather, which is the best, and also that there be no flue or nap that may be torn off when taking the watch out of the pocket. Cleanliness, too, is as needful here as in the key before winding; for, if there be dust or dirt in either instance, it will, you may rely upon it, work its way into the watch, as well as wear away the engine-turning of the case.

Waterproofing.

Porous goods are made waterproof according to two very distinct systems. According to the first the articles are made absolutely impervious to water and air by having their pores filled up with some oily or gummy substance, which becomes stiff and impenetrable. Caoutchouc, paints, oils, melted wax, etc., are of this kind. The other system consists in making the fabric *repellent* to water, while it remains quite porous and freely admits the passage of air. Goods so prepared will resist any ordinary rain, and we have seen a very porous fabric stretched over the mouth of a vessel and resist the passage of water one or two inches deep. The following recipes have been tried and found good. Most of those found in the recipe books are worthless.

To Render Leather Waterproof.—1. Melt together 2 oz. of Burgundy pitch, 2 oz. of soft wax, 2 oz. of turpentine, and 1 pint of raw linseed oil. Lay on with a brush while warm.

2. Melt 3 oz. lard and add 1 oz. powdered resin. This mixture remains soft at ordinary temperatures, and is an excellent application for leather.

Water-proof Canvas for Covering Carts, etc.—$9\frac{1}{2}$ gallons linseed oil, 1 lb. litharge, 1 lb. umber, boiled together for 24 hours. May be colored with any paint. Lay on with a brush.

To Make Sailcloth Impervious to Water, and yet Pliant and Durable.—Grind 6 lbs. English ochre with boiled oil, and add 1 lb. of black paint, which mixture forms an indifferent black. An ounce of yellow soap, dissolved by heat in half a pint of water, is mixed while hot with the paint. This composition is laid upon dry canvas as stiff as can conveniently be done with the brush. Two days after, a second coat of ochre and black paint (without any soap) is laid on, and, allowing this coat time to dry, the canvas is finished with a coat of any desired color. After three days it does not stick together when folded up. This is the formula used in the British navy yards, and it has given excellent results. We have seen a portable boat made of canvas prepared in this way and stretched on a skeleton frame.

Metallic Soap for Canvas.—The following is highly recommended as a cheap and simple process for coating canvas for wagon tops, tents, awnings, etc. It renders it impermeable to moisture, without making it stiff and liable to break. Soft soap is to be dissolved in hot water, and a solution of sulphate of iron added. The sulphuric acid combines with the potash of the soap, and the oxide of iron is precipitated with the fatty acid as insoluble iron soap. This is washed and dried, and mixed with linseed oil. The soap prevents the oil from getting hard and cracking, and at the same time water has no effect on it.

The following recipes are intended to be applied to woven fabrics, which they leave quite pervious to air but capable of resisting water.

1. Apply a strong solution of soap, not mere soap suds, to the wrong side of the cloth, and when dry wash the other side with a solution of alum.

2. The following recipe is substantially the same as the preceding, but if carefully followed in its details gives better results :

Take the material successively through baths of sulphate of alumina, of soap and of water ; then dry and smother or calender. For the alumina bath, use the ordinary neutral sulphate of alumina of commerce (concentrated alum cake), dissolving 1 part in 10 of water, which is easily done without the application of heat. The soap is best prepared in this manner : Boil 1 part of light resin, 1 part of soda crystals, and 10 of water, till the resin is dissolved ; salt the soap out by the addition of one-third part of common salt ; dissolve this soap with an equal amount of good palm oil soap (navy soap) in 30 parts of water. The soap bath should be kept hot while the goods are passing through it. It is best to have three vats along side of each other, and by a special arrangement to keep the goods down in the baths. Special care should be taken to have the fabric thoroughly soaked in the alumina bath.

3. Drs. Hager and Jacobsen remark that during the last

few years very good and cheap waterproof goods of this description have been manufactured in Berlin, which they believe is effected by steeping them first in a bath of sulphate of alumina and of copper, and then into one of water-glass and resin soap.

Whitewash.

The process of whitewashing is known by various names, such as "calcimining." "kalsomining," etc., most of them derived evidently from the latin name for *lime*, which was the principal ingredient of all the older forms of whitewash.

Professors of the "Art of Kalsomining" affect a great deal of mystery, but the process is very simple. It consists simply in making a whitewash with some neutral substance which is made to adhere by means of size or glue. It contains no caustic material like lime. Several substances have been used with good results. The best is zinc white. It gives the most brilliant effect but is the most expensive The next is Paris white or sulphate of baryta. This, when pure, is nearly equal to zinc white, but, unfortunately, common whiting is often sold for it, and more often mixed with it. It is not difficult, however, to detect common whiting either when alone or mixed with Paris white. When vinegar, or better still, spirits of salt, is poured on whiting, it foams or effervesces, but produces no effect on Paris white. Good whiting, however, gives very fair results and makes a far better finish than common lime as ordinarily used. When well made, however, good lime whitewash is very valuable for out-houses, and places where it is desirable to introduce a certain degree of disinfecting action. One of the best recipes for lime whitewash is that known as the "White House" whitewash, and sometimes called "Treasury Department" whitewash, from the fact that it is the recipe sent out by the Lighthouse Board of the Treasury Department. It has been found, by experience, to answer on wood, brick and stone, nearly as well as oil paint, and is much cheaper. Slake one-half bushel unslaked lime with boiling water, keeping it covered during the process. Strain it and add a peck of salt, dissolved in warm water; three pounds ground rice, put in boiling water and boiled to a thin paste; one-half pound powdered Spanish whiting and a pound of clear glue, dissolved in warm water;

mix these well together and let the mixture stand for several days. Keep the wash thus prepared in a kettle or portable furnace, and, when used, put it on as hot as possible with painters' or whitewash brushes.

Kalsomine, as distinguished from lime whitewash, is best suited for the interior of rooms in the dwelling house. To kalsomine a good sized room with two coats, proceed as follows :

Select some very clear colorless glue and soak ¼ lb. in water for 12 hours. Then boil it, taking great care that it does not burn, and this is best done by setting the vessel with the glue in a pan of water over the fire. When completely dissolved add it to a large pail of hot water, and into any desired quantity of this stir as much of the white material used as will make a cream. The quality of the resulting work will depend on the skill of the operator, but we may remark that it is easier to get a smooth hard finish by using three coats of thin wash than by using one coat of thick. If you have time for but one coat, however, you must give it body enough, In giving more than one coat let the last coat contain less glue than the preceding ones.

Kalsomine, such as we have described, may be colored by means of any of the cheap coloring stuffs.

The following is recommended as a good kalsomining fluid for walls : White glue, 1 pound ; white zinc, 10 pounds ; Paris white, 5 pounds ; water, sufficient. Soak the glue over night in three quarts of water, then add as much water again, and heat on a water bath till the glue is dissolved. In another pail put the two powders, and pour on hot water, stirring all the time, until the liquid appears like thick milk. Mingle the two liquids together. stir thoroughly, and apply to the wall with a whitewash brush.

It is often desirable to "kill" old whitewash, as it is called. as otherwise it would be impossible to get new whitewash or paper to stick to the walls. After scraping and washing off all lose material give the walls a thorough washing with a solution of sulphate of zinc (2 oz. to 1 gallon of water). The lime will be changed to plaster of Paris, and the zinc will be converted into zinc white, and if a coat of kalsomine be now given it will adhere very strongly and have great body.

Wood—Floors.

The following method of staining floors in oak or walnut colors is highly commended by the London *Furniture Gazette*: Put 1 oz. Vandyke brown in oil, 3 oz. pearlash, and 2 drms. dragon's blood, into an earthenware pan or large pitcher; pour on the mixture 1 quart of boiling water; stir with a piece of wood. The stain may be used hot or cold. The boards should be smoothed with a plane and glass-papered; fill up the cracks with plaster of Paris; the brush should not be rubbed across the boards, but lengthwise. Only a small piece should be done at a time. By rubbing on one place more than another an appearance of oak or walnut is more apparent; when quite dry, the boards should be sized with glue size, made by boiling glue in water, and brushing it in the boards hot. When this is dry, the boards should be papered smooth and varnished with brown hard varnish or oak varnish; the brown hard varnish will wear better and dry quicker; it should be thinned with a little French polish, and laid on the boards with a smooth brush.

Wax for Polishing Floors.—To prepare this, 12½ pounds yellow wax, rasped, are stirred into a hot solution of 6 pounds good pearlash, in rain water. Keeping the mixture well stirred while boiling, it is first quiet, but soon commences to froth; and when the effervescence ceases, heat is stopped, and there are added to the mixture, while still stirring, 6 pounds dry yellow ochre. It may then be poured into tin cans or boxes, and hardens on cooling. When wanted for use, a pound of it is diffused into 5 pints boiling hot water, and the mixture well stirred, applied while still hot to the floor by means of a paint brush. It dries in a few hours, after which the floor is to be polished with a large floor brush and afterwards wiped with a coarse woolen cloth. A coat of this wax will last six months.

Wood—Polishing.

Knotted or cross-grained wood cannot be planed with the planes used for deal, but with a special tool, of which the iron is placed at a more obtuse angle. These planes can be had in wood or metal, and are in general use by cabinet-makers. They are named according to the angle at which the iron is placed. For deal and soft wood this is 45 degrees, or York pitch; while the iron set at 55 degrees, middle pitch, or 60 degrees, half pitch, is used for molding planes for soft and hard wood. When the latter is, however, very knotty, it is worked over in all directions with a toothing plane, so as to cut across the fibres and reduce the surface to a general level. It is then finished by the scraper, often a piece of freshly broken glass, but more properly a thin plate of steel set in a piece of wood, and ground off quite square. The edge is then often rubbed with a burnisher, to turn up a slight wire edge. This will scrape down the surface of the wood until it is ready for " papering," *i. e.*, being further smoothed by glass or sandpaper. This is to be rubbed in all directions, until the work has an even surface, and the lines thus produced are further reduced by the finest sandpaper, marked 00. After this it is rubbed over with a bit of flannel, dipped in linseed oil, and allowed to dry. This oiling is then repeated, and the work again set aside for a day or more, until the oil is fairly absorbed.

If the wood be porous it must first be *filled*, as it is called, and for this nothing is better than whiting colored so as to resemble the wood and kept dry. Rub the wood with linseed oil and then sprinkle it with whiting. Rub the latter well in, wipe it off carefully and give time to dry. This is far superior to size.

The polish—French polish—is made by dissolving shellac in alcohol, methylated spirits, or even naphtha. This is facilitated by placing the jar or bottle in a warm place, on a stove or by the fire. Other gums are often added, but are not generally necessary. In short, no two polishers use precisely similar ingredients, but shellac is the base of all of them. The following recipes have been collected from various sources more or less reliable :

1. Shellac, 4 oz.; alcohol, 1 pint......2. Shellac, 4 oz.; sandarac, ½ oz.; alcohol, 1 pint.....3. Finishing polish : Alcohol (95 per cent.), ½ pint ; shellac, 2 dr.; gum benzoin, 2 dr.; put into a bottle, loosely corking it, and stand it near a fire, shaking it occasionally. When cold, add two teaspoonfuls of poppy oil, and shake well together.

These, it must be remembered, are polishes to be applied by means of rubbers, and not by a brush. Those used in the latter way are varnishes, such as are applied to cheap wares and also to parts of furniture and such articles as are carved and cannot in consequence be finished by rubbing.

The polisher generally consists of a wad of list rolled spirally, tied with twine and covered with a few thicknesses of linen rag. Apply a little varnish to the middle of the rubber and then enclose the latter in a soft linen rag folded twice. Moisten the face of the linen with a little raw linseed oil applied to the middle of it by means of the finger. Pass the rubber quickly and lightly over the surface of the work in small circular strokes until the varnish becomes nearly dry; charge the rubber with varnish again and repeat the rubbing till three coats are laid on, when a little oil may be applied to the rubber and two more coats given it. Proceed in this way until the varnish has acquired some thickness; then wet the inside of the linen cloth, before applying the varnish, with alcohol, and rub quickly, lightly and uniformly, the whole surface. Lastly, wet the linen cloth with a little oil and alcohol, without varnish, and rub as before till dry. Each coat is to be rubbed until the rag appears dry, and too much varnish must not be put on the rag at one time. Be also very particular to have the rags clean, as the polish depends in a great degree upon keeping everything free from dust and dirt.

To insure success the work must be done in a warm room, free from dust.

Turned articles must be brought to a fine smooth surface with the finest sandpaper, and the direction of the motion should be occasionally reversed so that the fibres which are laid down by rubbing one way may be raised up and cut off. To apply the polish, which is merely a solution of shellac in alcohol, take three or four thicknesses of linen rag and place a few drops of polish in the centre; lay over this a single thickness of linen rag and and a drop or two of raw linseed oil over the polish. The rubber is then applied with light friction over the entire surface of the work while revolving in the lathe, never allowing the hand or mandrel to remain still for an instant, so as to spread the varnish as evenly as possible, especially at the commencement, and paying particular attention to the internal angles, so as to prevent either deficiency or excess of varnish at those parts. The oil, in some degree, retards the evaporation of the spirit from the varnish and allows time for the process; it also presents a smooth surface and lessens the friction against the tender gum. When the varnish appears dry, a second, third and even further quantities are applied in the same manner, working, of course, more particularly upon those parts at all slighted in the earlier steps.

Wood—Staining.

In preparing any of the tinctures used for staining, it is of importance to powder or mash all the dry stuffs previous to dissolving or macerating them, and to purify all the liquids by filtration before use. Their coloring powers, which mainly depend on very accurate combinations of the requisite ingredients, should always be carefully tested before a free use is made of them, and the absorbent properties of the materials intended to be stained should be tested likewise. It will be better for inexperienced hands to coat twice or three times with a weak stain than only once with a very strong one, as by adopting the first mode a particular tint may be gradually effected, whereas, by pursuing the latter course, an irremediable discoloration may be the result. Coarse pieces of carving, spongy end, and cross-grained woods, should be previously prepared for the reception of stain; this is best done by putting on a thin layer of varnish, letting it dry, and then glass-papering it completely off again. Fine work merely requires to be oiled and slightly rubbed with the finest glass-paper. Thus prepared, the woody fibre is enabled to take on the stain more regularly, and to retain a high degree of smoothness. When stain is put on with a flat hog-hair tool, it is usually softened by a skilful but moderate application of a badger-hair softener. The steel comb is chiefly employed for streaking artificial oak, and the mottler is used for variegating and uniting the shades and tints of mahogany. Flannels and sponges are often used instead of brushes, but the implements most serviceable for veining or engraining purposes are small badger sash tools and sable pencils. The effect produced by a coat of stain cannot be ascertained until it has been allowed sufficient drying period.

This process may be used either for improving the natural color of wood or for changing it so completely as to give it the appearance of an entirely different kind of timber. Thus a light mahogany may be greatly improved by being made darker, and there are many other kinds of timber that are greatly improved by a slight change in their color. The following notes will be of use in the latter direction:

A solution of asphaltum in spirits of turpentine, makes a good brown stain for coarse oaken work, which is only intended to be varnished with boiled oil.

When discolored ebony has been sponged once or twice with a strong decoction of gall-nuts, to which a quantity of iron filings or rust has been added, its natural blackness becomes more intense.

The naturally pale ground and obscure grain of Honduras mahogany is often well brought out by its being coated first with spirits of hartshorn, and then with oil, which has been tinged with madder or venetian red.

Grayish maple may be whitened by carefully coating it with a solution of oxalic acid to which a few drops of nitric acid have been added.

Half a gallon of water in which ¼ lb. of oak bark and the same quantity of walnut shells or peels have been thoroughly boiled, makes an excellent improver of inferior rosewood; it is also far before any other of its kind for bringing out walnut.

Raw oil, mixed with a little spirits of turpentine, is universally allowed to be the most efficacious improver of the greater number of materials. Beautiful artificial graining may be imparted to various specimens of timber by means of a camel-hair pencil, with raw oil alone, that is, certain portions may be coated two or three times very tastefully, so as to resemble the rich varying veins which constitute the fibril figures; while the common, plain parts, which constitute the ground shades, may only be once coated with the oil, very much diluted with spirits of turpentine. The following are a few useful stains:

Mahogany.—1. Water, 1 gallon; madder, 8 oz.; fustic, 4 oz. Boil. Lay on with a brush while hot, and while wet streak it with black to vary the grain. This imitates Honduras mahogany.

2. Madder, 8 oz.; fustic, 1 oz.; logwood, 2 oz.; water, 1 gallon. Boil and lay on while hot. Resembles Spanish mahogany.

3. A set of pine shelves, which were brushed two or three times with a strong boiling decoction of logwood chips, and varnished with solution of shellac in alcohol, appear almost

like mahogany both in color and hardness. After washing with decoction of logwood and *drying thoroughly*, they received two coats of varnish. They were then carefully sand-papered and polished, and received a final coat of shellac varnish.

Imitation Ebony.—There are two processes in use for giving to very fine grained wood the appearance of ebony. One is a mere varnish, and may be applied in a few minutes, as it dries very rapidly. Either French polish, made black with any fine coloring matter, or good "air-drying black varnish," may be applied. This, however, gives only a superficial coloring, and when the edges and corners of the work wear off, the light-colored wood shows. The other method is as follows: Wash any compact wood with a boiling decoction of logwood three or four times, allowing it to dry between each application. Then wash it with a solution of acetate of iron, which is made by dissolving iron filings in vinegar. This stain is very black and penetrates to a considerable depth into the wood, so that ordinary scratching or chipping does not show the original color. Some recipes direct the solutions of logwood and iron to be mixed before being applied, but this is a great mistake.

Black Walnut Stain.—1. Take asphaltum, pulverize it, place it in a jar or bottle, pour over it about twice its bulk of turpentine, put it in a warm place, and shake it from time to time. When dissolved, strain it and apply it to the wood with a cloth or stiff brush. If it should make too dark a stain thin it with turpentine. This will dry in a few hours. If it is desired to bring out the grain still more, apply a mixture of boiled oil and turpentine; this is better than oil alone. Put no oil with the asphaltum mixture or it will dry very slowly. When the oil is dry the wood can be polished with the following: Shellac varnish, of the usual consistency, 2 parts; boiled oil, 1 part. Shake it well before using Apply it to the wood by putting a few drops on a cloth and rubbing briskly on the wood for a few moments. This polish works well on old varnished furniture.

2. The appearance of walnut may be given to white woods by painting or sponging them with a concentrated warm solution of permanganate of potassa. The effect is different on different kinds of timber, some becoming stained very rapidly, others requiring more time for the result. The per-

manganate is decomposed by the woody fibre; brown peroxide of manganese is precipitated, and the potash is afterwards removed by washing with water. The wood, when dry, may be varnished.

Brown Stain.—Paint over the wood with a solution made by boiling 1 part of catechu (cutch or gambier) with 30 parts of water and a little soda. This must be allowed to dry in the air, and then the wood is to be painted over with another solution made of 1 part of bichromate of potash and 30 parts of water. By a little difference in the mode of treatment and by varying the strength of the solutions, various shades of color may be given with these materials, which will be permanent and tend to preserve the wood.

Staining Oak.—According to Neidling, a beautiful orange-yellow tone, much admired in a chest at the Vienna Exhibition, may be imparted to oak wood by rubbing it in a warm room with a certain mixture until it acquires a dull polish, and then coating it after an hour with thin polish, and repeating the coating of polish to improve the depth and brilliancy of the tone. The ingredients for the rubbing mixture are about three ounces of tallow, three-fourths of an ounce of wax, add one pint of oil of turpentine, mixed by heating together and stirring.

Darkening Oak Framing.—Take one ounce of carbonate of soda, and dissolve in half pint boiling water; take a sponge or piece of clean rag, saturate it in the solution and pass gently over the wood to be darkened, so that it is wet evenly all over; let it dry for 24 hours. Try first on an odd piece of wood to see color; if too dark, make the solution weaker by adding more water; if not dark enough, give another coat. This may always be kept ready for use in a bottle corked up.

Imitation Rosewood.—Boil one-half pound of logwood in three pints of water till it is of a very dark red; add one-half ounce of salt of tartar. Stain the work with the liquor while it is boiling hot, giving three coats; then, with a painter's graining brush, form streaks with the following liquor: Boil one-half-pound of logwood chips in two quarts of water; add one ounce of pearlash, and apply hot,

Zinc.

Zinc, when cast into plates or ingots, is a brittle metal, easily broken by blows from a hammer. In this state it is evidently somewhat porous, as its specific gravity is only 6·8, while that of rolled zinc rises as high as 7·2. Zinc, when heated to 212° Fah., or over, becomes malleable and ductile, and when rolled into sheets it becomes exceedingly tough and does not regain its brittle character on cooling. Hence, sheet zinc has come into very extensive use in the arts.

To Pulverise Zinc.—Zinc becomes exceedingly brittle when heated to nearly its melting point. To reduce it to powder, therefore, the best plan is to pour melted zinc into a dry and warm cast-iron mortar, and as soon as it shows signs of solidifying pound it with the pestle. In this way it may be reduced to a very fine powder.

Black Varnish for Zinc.—Professor Böttger prepares a black coating for zinc by dissolving two parts nitrate of copper and three parts crystallized chloride of copper in sixty-four parts of water, and adding eight parts of nitric acid. This, however, is quite expensive; and in some places the copper salts are very difficult to obtain. On this account Puscher prepares black paint or varnish with the following simple ingredients: Equal parts of chlorate of potash and blue vitriol are dissolved in thirty-six times as much warm water, and the solution left to cool. If the sulphate of copper used contains iron, it is precipitated as a hydrated oxide, and can be removed by decantation or filtration. The zinc castings are then immersed for a few seconds in the solution until quite black, rinsed off with water, and dried. Even before it is dry, the black coating adheres to the object so that it may be wiped dry with a cloth. A more economical method, since a much smaller quantity of the salt solution is required, is to apply it repeatedly with a sponge. If copper-colored spots appear during the operation, the solution is applied to them a second time, and after a while they turn black. As soon as the object becomes equally black all over, it is washed with water and dried. On rubbing, the coating acquires a glittering appearance like indigo, which disappears on applying a few drops of linseed-oil varnish or "wax milk," and the zinc has then a deep black color and gloss.

INDEX.

Abyssinian gold, 9.
Accidents, general rules in case of, 9.
Acids, stains of, to remove, 130.
Adhesive paper, 101.
Alabaster, 11, 108.
    to work, 11.
    to polish, 11.
    to clean, 11.
    cement for, 12.
Albata, composition of, 13.
Alcohol for making varnish, 12.
    as a stimulant in cases of accident, 10.
Alloy for filling holes in cast iron, 13.
    for uniting iron, steel and brass, 13.
    general rules for making, 12.
Aluminium, bronze, 13.
    silver, 13.
Amalgam, Boettger's, 13.
    copper, 13.
    for silvering globes, etc., 13.
    for electrical machines, 13.
    silver, for mirrors, 98.
Amber, working and polishing, 15.
    cement for, 16.
    imitation, 16.
    solvents for, 119.
Aniline inks, 67.
    stains, to remove, 130.
Annealing copper, brass, etc., 16.
    steel, 133.
Anti-attrition lubricator, 90.
    metal, Babbitt's, 14.
Anti-friction metals, Belgian, 14.
    cheap, 14.
Antique bronze, 26.
Antiseptic preparations, 17.
Aquarium cement, 29.
Armenian cement, 29.
Arsenic, antidote for, 111.
Arsenical soap, 17.
    powder, 17.
Axle grease, Booth's, 90.
Babbitt metal, how to make and apply, 14.
Balls for removing grease, 131.
Barometer paper, 102.
Basketware, varnish for, 139.
Batteries, voltaic, 145.
    zincs for, 146.
    connections for, 145.
Beeswax, to bleach, 17.
Belgian antifriction metals, 14.
Belting, leather, cement for, 35.
Bengal light, 84.

Blackboards, to make, 18.
    crayons for, 40.
Blazing off steel springs, 134.
Bleaching by means of sulphur, 137.
    ivory, 78.
    shellac, 122.
    skeleton leaves, 84.
Blue color, to remove from iron and steel, 76.
Blue light, 84, 86.
Bluing of steel, 136.
Booth's axle grease, 90.
Boxes, metal for lining, 14.
Brass, 18.
    to finish, 19.
    to color and varnish, 19.
    to bronze, 19, 25.
    to blacken, 20.
    to whiten, 21.
    to deposit by electricity, 21.
    to coat with copper, 22.
    to coat with silver, 126.
    to clean, 22.
    to lacquer, 22.
Brazing, 22.
Brightening iron, 76.
British plate, composition of, 13
Bronze, aluminium, 13.
Bronze for brass, 25.
    antique, 26, 105.
Bronzing, 25.
Bronzing liquid, 26.
Bronzing wood, leather, paper, etc., 26.
Browning gun barrels, 60.
Browning mixture for gun barrels, 60.
Buckland's cement, 29.
Buffing metals, etc., 94, 95.
Burnishing metals, 94.
Burns, cure for, 27.
Calcimine, 149.
Canvas, to make waterproof, 147.
    metallic soap for, 148.
Cap cement, Faraday's, 31.
Carmine ink, French process for making, 67.
Case-hardening iron, 73.
Casein and soluble glass cement, 30.
Casein Mucilage, 30.
Cast steel—see steel.
Catgut, how to make, 27.
Cats, to cure skins of, 129.
Cement for alabaster, 12.
    aquarium, 29.

Cement, Armenian, 29.
    Buckland's, 29.
    cheese, 30.
    Chinese (schio-liao), 30.
    Faraday's cap, 31.
    electrical, 31.
    for glass, earthenware, etc., 31.
    glass, 31.
    gutta percha, 33.
    iron, for pipes, etc., 33.
    Japanese, 34.
    for kerosene oil lamps, 34.
    labels, 34.
    for uniting leather and metal,
    for leather belting, 35.
    litharge and glycerine, 35.
    for attaching metal to glass, 36.
    Paris, for shells, etc., 36.
    porcelain, 37.
    soft, 37.
    soluble glass, 37.
    Sorel's, 38.
    steam boiler, 38.
    transparent, 38.
    turner's, 38.
    Wollaston's, 38.
    sulphur, 138.
Cements, general rules for using, 28.
Chalk for polishing, 114.
    prepared, 114.
Chatham light, 89.
Cheese cement, 30.
Chinese cement, 30.
    glue, 30.
Chlorate of potassa, caution, 87.
Cleaning engravings, etc., 105.
    glass, 57.
    glass for mirrors, 97.
    looking glasses, 99.
    ivory, 78.
    marble, 91.
    silver, 125.
Cliché metal, 15.
Cloth, to make waterproof, 147.
Clothes on fire, what to do, 48.
Cock metal, 13.
Coffee as a stimulant in case of accident, 10.
Cold process for zincing iron, 75.
    tinning iron, 75.
Color of tempered steel, 134.
Connections for voltaic batteries, 145.
Copal, solvents for, 119.
Copper, 38.
    amalgam, how to make, 13.
    to polish, 38.
    to weld, 39.
Coppering iron or steel, 39.

Coral, artificial, 40.
Cork, to cut, 40.
    to make airtight, 40.
Corrosive sublimate, antidote for, 112.
Crayons, for blackboards, 40.
    to preserve, 41.
Creases, to take out of engravings, etc., 102.
Crocus martis, for polishing, 115.
Curing and tanning skins, 128.
Curling metal surfaces, 41.
Cuticle, liquid, 41.
Dammar, solvents for, 119.
Demons, tableaux light for, 86.
Dials, painting hours on, 101.
Diamond for drilling glass, 56.
Disinfecting by sulphur vapors, 137.
    by pastils, etc., 50.
Drawing paper, size for, 127.
    to mount, 102.
Dresses, how to make fire-proof, 48.
Drilling glass, 55.
Dumoulin's liquid glue, 32.
Ebony, imitation, 156.
Electrical amalgam, 13.
    Boettger's, 13.
Electrical cement, 31.
Electrum, composition of, 13.
Elemi, solvents for, 119.
Elutriation, how to perform, 113.
Engravings, to take creases out of, 102.
    to take water stains out of, 105.
Eraser for ink, 70.
Etching copper, 42.
    varnish for, 42.
    acid for, 42.
    steel, liquid for, 43.
    glass, 44.
Eye, accidents to, 44.
    to remove particles from, 45
    lime in, 46.
Faraday's cap cement, 31.
Fire-proof dresses, 48.
Fire, clothes on, 48.
Fires, to prevent, 46.
    what to do in case of, 47.
Fluxes for solders, 24.
Fly papers, to make, 49.
Forging iron, 72.
French polish, 152.
Freezing mixtures, various kinds, 50.
Freezing, to prevent ink from, 69.
Fruit stains, to remove, 130.
Fuller's earth for scouring, 131.
Fumigating pastils, how to make and use, 50.
Furs, skins, curing, 128.

INDEX. 161

Fusible metals, how to make and use, 15.
Ghosts, tableaux light for, 86.
Gilded ware, cleaning, 80.
Gilding metals, best methods, 51.
    with gold leaf, 52.
    picture frames, 52.
    wood, 54.
    steel, 54.
Glass, soluble, cement, 30.
    cement, 31.
    earthenware, etc., cement for, 31.
    working, 54.
    cutting, 54.
    cutting without a diamond, 55.
    drilling, 55.
    how to turn and bore in a lathe, 55.
    stoppers, fitting, 56.
    stoppers, to remove, when tight, 56.
    to powder, 57.
    ground, to imitate, 57.
    vessels, to cleanse, 57.
    paper, 103.
    paper, waterproof, 103.
Glassware, to pack, 59.
Glue, how to choose, 31.
    how to prepare, 32.
    Chinese, 30.
    liquid, 32.
    marine, 35.
    mouth, 33.
    portable, 33.
Gold, Abyssinian, 9.
    gilding with, 52.
    ink, 68.
    lacquer, 82.
    size, preparation of, 127.
Grass, dried, to stain, 59.
Grease stains, to remove, 130.
Green light, 85, 86.
Ground glass, to imitate, 57.
Guns, to improve the shooting of, 59.
    to keep barrels from rusting, 60.
    to brown the barrels of, 60.
    varnish for barrels, 61.
Gutta percha cement, 33.
Gypsum, 108.

Handles of knives to fasten, 62.
Hard solder, 23.
Hardening copper, brass, etc., 16.
    steel, 133.
Heat used in forging iron, 72.
Hygrometric or barometer paper, 102.

Indelible aniline ink, 68.
    Indian ink, 68.
Indestructible ink, 69.
Indian ink, how to choose, 63.

Ink, different kinds of, 62.
    rules for selecting and using, 63.
    black, recipe for, 66.
    Runge's black ink, 66.
    blue ink, 66.
    carmine ink, French process, 67.
    red ink, 67.
    aniline inks, general formula, 67.
    aniline ink, violet, 67.
    aniline ink, blue, 67.
    aniline inks, aqueous solutions, 67.
    gold, 68.
    silver, 68.
    marking ink for linen, 68.
    indelible aniline, 68.
    indelible Indian, 68.
    indestructible, 69.
    that will not freeze, 69.
    sympathetic or secret, 69.
    eraser, 70.
    pencils, 106.
    stains, to remove from silver, 125.
    stains, to remove, 131.
Inks for rubber stamps and stencils, 70.
Inlaying, simple method of, 71.
    imitation, 71.
Iron cement for joints, 33.
    forging, different heats employed for, 72.
    welding, 72.
    case hardening, 73.
    rust, to prevent, 74.
    zincing, 74.
    cold process for zincing, 75.
    tinning, 75.
    tinning in the cold, 75.
    brightening, 76.
    to remove blue color from, 76.
    mould, to remove, 131.
    and tin, alloys of, 139.
Ivory, character of as regards work, 76.
    working and polishing, methods for, 77.
    bleaching and cleaning, 78.
Ivy, poisoning with, remedy, 113.

Japanese cement, 34.
Javelle water, 79.
Jewelry, cleaning, 80.

Kalsomine, 149.
Kerosene oil lamps, cement for, 34.

Labels, cement for, 34.
Lac, different kinds of, 121.
Lacquer, method of using, 81.
    deep gold, 82.
    bright gold, 82.
    pale gold, 82.
    used by A. Ross, 82,

Lacquer, preservation of, 83.
Laundry gloss, 83.
Leather belting, cement for, 35.
Leather and metal, cement for, 35.
Leather, to make waterproof, 147.
Leaves, skeleton, 83.
Lights, signal and colored, 84.
   Bengal, 84.
   blue, 84, 86.
   red, 85, 86.
   white, 85, 86.
   crimson fire, 85.
   green, 85, 86.
   for indoor illumination, 85.
   phosphorous, 88.
   photographic, 88.
   Chatham, 89.
Litharge and glycerine cement, 35.
Looking glasses, care of, 99.
   how to clean, 99.
Lubricators, rules for selecting, 89.
   plumbago, 90.
   anti-attrition, 90.
   fine lubricating oil, 90.
   Booth's axle grease, 90.
Magnesium light, 85.
Mahogany, to improve, 155.
   artificial, 155.
Maple, to whiten, 155.
Maps, varnish for, 141.
Marble, composition of, 90.
   method of working, 91.
   method of polishing, 92.
   substances which injure it, 91.
   to clean, 91.
   sculpture, how finished, 93.
Marine glue, 35.
Marking ink, 68.
Mastic, solvents for, 119.
Mats, skins cured for, 128.
Mercury, bichloride or corrosive sublimate, 112.
Metal, fusible, 15.
   anti-friction, 14.
   Babbitt, 14.
Metal, to attach to glass, 36.
Metallic soap for canvas, 148.
Metals, to polish, 94, 95, 96.
Metals, bright, painting, 101.
Mexican onyx, 90.
Mildew, to remove, 131.
Mirrors, to make, 96.
   for optical purposes, 96.
   silver amalgam for, 98.
   care of, 99.
Mono-chromatic light, 86.
Moulds made of sulphur, 138.
Mouth glue, 33.

Mucilage, casein, 30.
Murderers, tableaux, light for, 86.
Newton's fusible metal, 15.
Nickel, characters of, 99.
   to deposit without battery, 100.
Noise, prevention of, 100.
Novargent, 126.
Oak, to stain, 157.
   to darken, 157.
Oil, fine, for lubricating, 90.
Oilstone powder for polishing, 116.
Onion's fusible metal, 15.
Opium poisoning, remedy for, 112.
Oriental alabaster, 11.
Oxidized silver, 123.
Paint, to remove stains of, 132.
Painting bright metals, 101.
Painting metal dials, 101.
Paper, various uses of, 101.
   adhesive, 101.
   barometer, 102.
   creases, to take out of, 102.
   drawing, to mount, 102.
   glass paper, 103.
   to prepare for varnishing, 103.
   pollen powder or paper powder, 104.
   tracing, 104.
   transfer, 104.
   to remove water stains from, 105.
   waxed, 105.
   for pillows, 107.
   size for, 127.
Paris cement for shells, etc., 36.
Paris green, antidote for, 111.
Paste, recipes for, 36.
Pastils, fumigating, 50.
Patina or artificial bronze, 105.
Patterns, to trace, 105.
Pencil marks, to fix, 106.
Pencils, ink, to make, 106.
Peroxide of iron for polishing, 116.
Pewter, 15, 107.
   hardened, 107.
   for caps and polishing tools, 107.
Phosphorous light, 88.
Phosphorous as poison, antidote, 112.
Photographic light, 88.
Pillows for sick room, 107.
Plaster-of-Paris, preparation of, 108.
   to harden, 108.
   to cast, 108.
Plate renovator, 126.
Plating without battery, 126.
   nickel, 100.
Platinum, solder for, 25.
Plumbago as a lubricator, 90.
Poisons, cautions in regard to, 109.

INDEX. 163

Poisons, acids, 110.
   oxalic acid, 110.
   Prussic acid, 111.
   arsenic or Paris green, 111.
   corrosive sublimate, 112.
   phosphorous, 112.
   opium, 112.
   strychnine, 113.
   ivy poisoning, 113.
   stings, 113.
Polishing smoothing irons, 83.
   metals, 94.
   powders, selection of, 113.
   elutriation of, 113.
   chalk or whiting, 114.
   prepared chalk, 114.
   crocus or rouge, 115.
   Andrew Ross's mode of preparing, 115.
   oilstone powder, 116.
   pumice-stone powder, 116.
   putty powder, 117.
   Vienna lime, 118.
Polishing powder, Lord Ross's mode of preparing, 116.
Polishing powders, oilstone powder, 116.
   pumice-stone powder, 117.
   putty powder, 117.
   Vienna lime, 118.
Polishing-wood, 151.
   in the lathe, 153.
Pollen powder or paper, 104.
Porcelain cement, 37.
Powders, polishing, 113.
Printing in gold, silver and bronze, 52.
Prussic acid, antidote for, 111.
Pumice-stone powder, 117.
Putty powder for polishing, 117.

Queen's metal, composition of, 15.

Rabbits, to cure skins of, 129.
Red ink, 67.
Red light, 85, 86.
Resins, characters of, 119.
Rosewood, imitation, 157.
Ross, Andrew, lacquer used by, 82.
   method of preparing rouge for polishing, 115.
   method of preparing putty powder, 118.
Ross, Lord, method of preparing rouge for polishing, 116.
Rouge for polishing, 115.
Rust and corrosion of iron, to prevent, 74.

Sailcloth, to make impervious to water, 147.
Sandarach, solvents for, 119.
Saws, how to put in order, 120.
Saws, tempering, 135.

Secret writing, ink for, 69.
Seed lac, 121
Sheep skins for mats, curing of, 128.
Shellac, character of, 121.
   adulteration of, 121.
   solvents for, 119, 121.
   clarifying solutions of, 122.
   bleaching, 122.
   varnish, 142.
Sieves, very fine, to make, 128.
Silver, aluminium, 13.
   characters of, 122.
   for solder, 23.
   ink, 68.
   amalgam for mirrors, 98.
   how hardened, 122.
   oxidized, 123.
   to clean, 125.
   to imitate old, 124.
   to remove ink stains from, 125.
   to dissolve off plated ware, 125.
   to work and polish, 122.
   nitrate, to remove stains of, 132.
Silvering mirrors, amalgam for, 96.
   inside of globes, etc., 13.
   leather, etc., 126.
   powder, 126.
   solution, 127.
   amalgam for metals, 127.
Silversmiths' work, how finished, 122.
Size, glue, how to make, 127.
   for window shades, 129.
   for drawing paper, 127.
   gold, 127.
Sizing for window shades, 127.
Skeleton leaves, 83.
Skins, tanning and curing, 128.
Skins, sheep, curing for mats, 128.
   of rabbits, cats, etc., to cure, 129.
Soft cement, 37.
Solder, soft, composition of, 23.
   hard, how to make, 24.
   flux for, 24.
   wire, 24.
   for platinum, 25.
   German silver, 25.
Soldering, 22
Soldering fluid, 23.
Soluble glass cement, 37.
Sorel's cement, 38.
Speculum metal, how to make, 15.
Spirituous liquors as a stimulant, 10.
Spotted varnish, to restore, 145.
Springs, to temper, 135.
Staining wood, 154.
Stains, how removed, 129.
   acids, 129.
   aniline dyes, 130.

INDEX.

Stains, fruit, 130.
    grease, 130.
    ink and iron mould, 131.
    mildew, 131.
    nitrate of silver, 132.
    paint, 132.
    tar, 132.
Stamps, ink for, 70.
Steam boiler cement, 38.
Steel, forging, 132.
    burnt, to restore, 133.
    to gild, 54.
    to harden, 133.
    to temper, 134.
    blazing off, 134.
    welding, 136.
    to blue, 136.
    springs, to temper, 135.
Stencils, ink for, 70.
Stick lac, 121.
Stimulants, use of in case of accident, 10.
Stings of insects, remedy for, 113.
Stoppers, glass, to fit, 56.
    to remove tight, 56.
Strychnine as a poison, antidote for, 13.
Sulphur, 137.
    bleaching by means of, 137.
    disinfecting by means of, 137.
    as a cement, 138.
    for making moulds, 138.
Sympathetic ink, 69.
Tanning and curing skins, 128.
Tar, to remove stains of, 132.
Tempering steel on one edge, 134.
    steel, color indications, 134.
    steel springs, 135.
    steel saws, 135.
Tin, 138.
    how corroded, 138.
    alloys of, 138.
    and iron, 139.
Tinning iron, 75.
Tracing paper, 104.
Transfer paper, 104.
Transparent cement for glass, 38.
Turner's cement, 38.
Tutty powder or putty powder, 117.
Type metal, 15.
Varnish, 139.
    for browned iron, 61.
    for basket ware, 139.
    black, for optical work, 140.
    black, for cast iron, 140.
    green, 140.
    for bright iron work, 141.
    for maps, 141.
    mastic, 141.

Varnish for bright metals, 141.
    for paintings, 141.
    for preventing rust, 142.
    shellac, 142.
    tortoise shell, Japan, 142.
    turpentine, 142.
    for violins and similar articles, 142.
    for replacing turpentine and linseed oil paints, 142.
    white, hard, for wood or metal, 143.
    white, for paper, 143.
    white spirit, 143.
    Parisian, for wood, 143.
    for stained wood, 143.
    to restore spotted, 145.
    black, for zinc, 158.
Varnishing paper, 103.
    directions for, 144.
Vienna lime for polishing, 118.
Violins, varnish for, 142.
Voltaic batteries, 145.
    zincs for, 146.

Walnut, black, to imitate, 156.
Washing glass vessels, 58.
Watch, care of, 146.
Waterproof glass paper, 103.
Waterproofing, methods used for, 147.
    for leather, 147.
    for canvas, 147.
    for sailcloth, 147.
    ordinary goods, 148.
Water stains, to remove from engravings, 105.
Wax for polishing floors, 151.
Waxed paper, 105.
Weather paper or barometer paper, 102.
Welding copper, 39.
    iron, 72.
    steel, 136.
Whiting for polishing, 114.
White light, 85, 86, 87.
Whitewash, Treasury Department recipe for, 149.
Whitewash, to "kill," 150.
Window shades, sizing for, 127.
Wollaston's white cement, 38.
Wood's fusible metal, 15.
Wood floors, 151.
    polishing, 151.
    staining, 154.

Zinc, characters of, 158.
    to pulverize, 158.
    black varnish for, 158.
Zincing iron, 74.
    iron by cold process, 75.
Zincs for batteries, amalgamating, 146

A NEW SERIES OF PRACTICAL BOOKS.

WORK MANUALS.

The intention of the publishers is to give in this Series a number of small books which will give Thorough and Reliable Information in the plainest possible language, upon the

ARTS OF EVERYDAY LIFE.

Each volume will be by some one who is not only practically familiar with his subject, but who has the ability to make it clear to others. The volumes will each contain from 50 to 75 pages, will be neatly and clearly printed on good paper and bound in tough and durable binding. The price will be *25 cents each, or five for One Dollar.*

The following are the titles of the volumes already issued. Others will follow at short intervals.

I. Cements and Glue.

A Practical Treatise on the Preparation and Use of All Kinds of Cements, Glue and Paste. By JOHN PHIN, Editor of the *Young Scientist* and the *American Journal of Microscopy*

Every mechanic and householder will find this volume of almost everyday use. It contains nearly 200 recipes for the preparation of Cements for almost every conceivable purpose

II. The Slide Rule, and How to Use It.

This is a compilation of Explanations, Rules and Instructions suitable for mechanics and others interested in the industrial arts. Rules are given for the measurement of all kinds of boards and planks, timber in the round or square, glaziers' work and painting, brickwork, paviors' work, tiling and slating, the measurement of vessels of various shapes, the wedge, inclined planes, wheels and axles, levers, the weighing and measurement of metals and all solid bodies, cylinders, cones, globes, octagon rules and formulæ, the measurement of circles, and a comparison of French and English measures, with much other information, useful to builders, carpenters, bricklayers, glaziers, paviors, slaters, machinists and other mechanics.

Possessed of this little Book and a good Slide Rule, mechanics might carry in their pockets some hundreds of times the power of calculation that they now have in their heads, and the use of the instrument is very easily acquired

III. Hints for Painters, Decorators and Paperhangers.

Being a selection of Useful Rules, Data, Memoranda, Methods and Suggestions for House, Ship, and Furniture Painting, Paperhanging, Gilding, Color Mixing, and other matters Useful and Instructive to Painters and Decorators. Prepared with Special Reference to the Wants of Amateurs. By an Old Hand.

IV. Construction, Use and Care of Drawing Instruments.

Being a Treatise on Draughting Instruments, with Rules for their Use and Care, Explanations of Scales, Sectors and Protractors. Together with Memoranda for Draughtsmen, Hints on Purchasing Paper, Ink, Instruments, Pencils, etc. Also a Price List of all materials required by Draughtsmen. Illustrated with twenty-four Explanatory Illustrations. By FRED. T. HODGSON.

V. The Steel Square.

Some Difficult Problems in Carpentry and Joinery Simplified and Solved by the aid of the Carpenters' Steel Square, together with a Full Description of the Tool, and Explanations of the Scales, Lines and Figures on the Blade and Tongue, and How to Use them in Everyday Work. Showing how the Square may be Used in Obtaining the Lengths and Bevels of Rafters, Hips, Groins, Braces, Brackets, Purlins, Collar-Beams, and Jack-Rafters. Also, its Application in Obtaining the Bevels and Cuts for Hoppers, Spring Mouldings, Octagons, Diminished Styles, etc., etc. Illustrated by Numerous Wood-cuts By FRED. T. HODGSON, Author of the 'Carpenters' Steel Square."

Note.—This work is intended as an elementary introduction for the use of those who have not time to study Mr. Hodgson's larger work on the same subject.